IN THE LAND OF
TEMPLE CAVES

IN THE LAND OF TEMPLE CAVES

From St. Emilion to Paris's St. Sulpice

Notes on Art and the Human Spirit

FREDERICK TURNER

COUNTERPOINT

A MEMBER OF THE PERSEUS BOOKS GROUP

NEW YORK

Text design by Jeff Williams

Library of Congress Cataloging-in-Publication Data

Turner, Frederick W., 1937-
    In the land of the temple caves : notes on art and the
human spirit / Frederick Turner.
        p. cm.
    Includes bibliographical references (p. 197).
    ISBN 1-58243-266-x (alk. paper)
    1. Art—Philosophy. 2. Aesthetics. 3. Turner, Frederick W.,
1937—Travel—France. 4. Art, Prehistoric—France.
5. France—Description and travel. I. Title.
    N70.T93 2440
    700'.1—DC22

                                                    2003025008

For

JOHN HARLAND HICKS

EXTRACTS
(*After Melville*)

Very deep is the well of the past. Should we not call it bottomless?
Bottomless indeed, if–and perhaps only if–the past we mean is the past
merely of the life of mankind, that riddling essence of which our own
normally unsatisfied and quite abnormally wretched existences form a
part; whose mystery, of course, includes our own. . . . For the deeper we
sound, the further down into the lower world of the past we probe and
press, the more do we find that the earliest foundations of humanity, its
history and culture, reveal themselves unfathomable. No matter to what
hazardous lengths we let out our line they still withdraw again, and further, into the depths.

> —THOMAS MANN,
> *Joseph and His Brothers*

Let us . . . work and wedge our feet downward through the mud and
slush of opinion, and prejudice, and tradition, and delusion, and
appearance, that alluvion which covers the globe . . . till we come to a
hard bottom and rocks in place, which we can call *reality*, and say, This is,
and no mistake. . . .

> —HENRY DAVID THOREAU,
> *Walden*

Time is the stream I go a-fishing in. . . .

> —THOREAU,
> *Walden*

Death is the mother of beauty. . . .

> —WALLACE STEVENS,
> "Sunday Morning"

. . . endocranial casts of the earliest and lowliest Hominidae permit us
the respectable guess that the capacity to symbolize, to mythologize, to
speak genuine language belonged already to those early levels of human-
ization. . . . If so, then mythopoea is coeval with humanity and indeed an
aspect of human morphology.

> —EARL W. COUNT,
> "Myth as World View"

Art, poetry, and music are matters of survival. They are guardians and markers of what's oldest and first in the human spirit.

> —SIR LAURENS VAN DE POST,
> in a late interview

Covering a period of almost 20,000 years . . . this complex body of cave art is the most ancient, continuous, and possibly the most revealing product of human creation.

> —PAUL SHEPARD,
> *The Tender Carnivore & The Sacred Game*

Anything we can think of as the source and mother of our feelings is art. Anything that isn't isn't.

> —GIANFRANCO BARUCHELLO,
> *How to Imagine*

The very language we use to discuss the past speaks of tools, hunters, and of *men*, when every statue and painting we discover cries out to us that this Ice Age humanity was a culture of art, the love of animals, and women.

> —WILLIAM IRWIN THOMPSON,
> *The Time Falling Bodies Take to Light*

And the whole of the soul . . .
Still hankers after lions . . .

> —WALLACE STEVENS,
> "Lions in Sweden"

Jupiter shortened the springtime which had prevailed of old, and instituted a cycle of four seasons in the year, winter, summer, changeable autumn, and a brief spring. Then, for the first time, the air became parched and acrid, and glowed with white heat, then hanging icicles formed under the chilling blasts of the wind. It was in those days that men first sought covered dwelling places: they made their homes in caves and thick shrubberies, or bound branches together with bark.

> —OVID,
> *Metamorphoses*

From Naxos (Dionysus) came to Argos and punished Perseus, who at first opposed him . . . by inflicting a madness on the Argive women: they began devouring their own infants raw. Perseus hastily admitted his error, and appeased Dionysus by building a temple in his honour.

—ROBERT GRAVES,
The Greek Myths

All things change, but nothing dies: the spirit wanders hither and thither, taking possession of what limbs it pleases, passing from beasts into human bodies, or again our human spirit passes into beasts, but never at any time does it perish.

—OVID,
Metamorphoses

My soul turns into a tree,
And an animal, and a cloud bank.
Then changed and odd it comes home
And asks me questions. What should I reply?

—HERMAN HESSE,
"Sometimes"

The natural world is a spiritual house, where the pillars that are alive
Let slip at times some strangely garbled words;
Man walks there through forests of physical things that are also
    spiritual things,
That watch him with affectionate looks.

—CHARLES BAUDELAIRE,
"Intimate Associations"

What leaf-fring'd legend haunts about thy shape
  Of deities or mortals, or of both,
    In Tempe or the dales of Arcady?
  What men or gods are these?

—JOHN KEATS
"Ode on a Grecian Urn"

   . . . by the Auvézère
Poppies and day's eyes and the green émail
    Rose over us; and we knew that stream,
And our two horses had traced the valleys;
Knew how the low flooded lands squared out with poplars,
In the young days when the deep sky befriended.

—EZRA POUND,
"Near Périgord"

Do you know what the earth
Meditates upon in autumn?

> —PABLO NERUDA,
> *The Book of Questions*

. . . at no other time (than autumn) does the earth let itself be inhaled in
one smell, the ripe earth; in a smell that is in no way inferior to the
smell of the sea, bitter where it borders on taste, and more honeysweet
where you feel it touching the first sounds. Containing depth within
itself, darkness, something of the grave almost.

> —RAINER MARIA RILKE,
> *Letters on Cézanne*

I have made this poem for you, that men may read it
Before they read of Gorgael and Dectora,
As men in the old times, before the harps began,
Poured out wine for the high invisible ones.

> —W. B. YEATS,
> *"Introductory Lines"*

No man can afford to dispense with debilitating pleasures; no ascetic
can be considered reliably sane. Hitler was the archetype of the
abstemious man. When the other krauts saw him drink water in the Beer
Hall they should have known he was not to be trusted.

> —A. J. LIEBLING,
> *Between Meals*

For each of us then, as we pass from nonbeing into being, there moves
with us like the tail of a comet, as we enter into our perihelion of the
present, remembrances of infinitudes of time-past. This is memory of a
strange sort–memory manifested in biochemical energy.

> —JOHN N. BLEIBTREU,
> *The Parable of the Beast*

The mission of man on earth is to remember. To remember to remember.

> —HENRY MILLER,
> *Remember to Remember*

CONTENTS

Preface XIII

Maps XIX

St.-Emilion 1

Time Travel 8

Art and Crisis 12

In the Cave of the Hundred Mammoths 26

Tasting the Past 41

Venus and the Castle 44

Life Against Death 59

Balance 68

Oradour-sur-Glane 81

XII — *Contents*

Dream of the Mythic Past 92

The Mark of the Bear 108

La Ferrassie 116

The Weight of the Past 138

Balzac Versus Hitler 153

Degenerate Art 165

Reading a Forgotten Language 173

In the Hall of the Past 181

St.-Sulpice 189

Acknowledgements 195

References 197

PREFACE

In the immediate aftermath of the attacks on America in September 2001, I felt my emotional and spiritual foundations had been profoundly shaken—though unlike the towers and the wall of the Pentagon, they had not collapsed. Of course, I had a great deal of company. The naked daring of the attacks and the symbolism of their targets shocked millions around the world and temporarily at least humbled the mightiest nation on earth.

My reaction, if there was anything at all singular about it, was only slightly different in nature. As a writer and Sunday painter I had spent most of my life braced and buttressed by the belief that Art, broadly conceived, was humanity's fullest expression of itself as well as its most beautiful aspiration toward divinity. But what could paintings say about such terrible acts of destruction? How could the words of books help us to comprehend the motives of those who evidently hated so much of what the West stood for? How could a Chopin étude stand up to the thunderous collapse of the proud towers? With the nation vowing vengeance, girding for war, and with our politicians urging all of the West to join in, Art suddenly seemed only a harmless decoration at best, a useless distraction at worst.

But a man of my years doesn't easily give up the things he's lived by. As I make clear in the opening pages of this book, I eventually came to feel that it was necessary for me to go back to the very beginnings of Art and try to assess anew its meanings in the long human story. This meant a personal investigation of what the great mythographer Joseph Campbell felicitously called the "temple caves," those sanctuaries in France and Spain, the earliest known one of which contains decorations more than 32,000 years old. What did it mean that humans at so ancient a date were already capable of producing art of great power and technical sophistication? Here in the temple caves were works more advanced than the hunting implements by which those people had lived.

Plainly for this kind of thing no mere armchair investigation would do. No, I would have to go there, to the literal ground of the beginnings. I would have to see the art in its natural settings. I would have to see the conformations of the caves, the traces of the mighty rivers of the Ice Age, the way the ice caps had scoured and sculpted the land in their successive advances and slow retreats. I would have to feel the quality of the soil, handle its stones, gaze upon the sloping ranks of the vineyards and orchards that had succeeded the landscape of the great herds and their human hunters. And after months of armchair preparation that is what I did in

September and October 2002. This book describes what I found there—which inevitably is more than what I merely saw. No meaningful journey is ever quite what you thought it would be when you embarked on it—and shouldn't be. Your physical departure, in other words, often is accompanied by a psychological and spiritual one as well, leaving you open to revelation, epiphanies large and small, surprise, and the revisitation of the past as offered by your encounters with the new in the present. Perhaps the fact that I began my quest in St.-Emilion at the gateway to the country of the caves, yet ended it in Paris's Place St.-Sulpice—definitely not on my itinerary—sufficiently suggests the mysterious workings of this process.

Several caveats now.

First, this is not a book for specialists. I make no pretense to being a paleoanthropologist. Such men and women, as well as anthropologists and art historians, may find my treatment of such hotly contested issues as the nature of the Neanderthals, their relations with the Cro-Magnons, the economic specifics of Ice Age hunting cultures, and the stylistic development of cave art done with a broad brush. I didn't want to try to become a specialist in any of the tangled fields across which I felt I needed to trespass, vainly attempting to sort through intense scholarly debates. Entire careers, lifetimes really, have been spent parsing these ancient mysteries. And in any case, in these fields today's absolute proof often turns out to be tomorrow's discarded speculation. Moreover, no one can say what the picture of Ice Age art and culture will look like a century from now, for just as the discoveries at Lascaux in 1940 and Chauvet in 1994 revolutionized our sense of the deep past, so we must confidently assume that further exciting discoveries await us and that these will significantly alter and enrich our understanding. Therefore, like a traveler off the beaten track I had to trust my instincts in where I needed to go, remembering as I went that this was after all my quest, not another's. For those non-specialists who wish to make their own trespasses I append a reference section to these pages.

Second, this isn't a travel book in the generally accepted sense of the term. Readers expecting a straight-ahead guide to the caves are bound to find this book filled with annoying divagations and detours into regions seemingly far removed from the caves themselves. I make no apology for this; it is the nature of the journey I made. Nor can I truly apologize for the continuous presence in these pages of those guides who have been with me for so many years—Keats and Thoreau, Rilke and Henry Miller—none of whom, so far as I know, had anything to say about the caves, though they had a great deal to say about Art. These are the writers who have shown me best how to get to places that aren't down on any map, planned for in any itinerary.

This brings me to my final caveat, the map. Try as I might, I couldn't find a cartographical designation for the territory I traversed during those golden weeks in France. The majority of the important cave sites I visited were in the *département* of the Dordogne. But I also had significant moments outside the Dordogne: in the Tarn-et-Garonne in the south; in the Corréze to the east; and the Haute-Vienne in the north. There isn't any

Région that covers all this, either. Aquitaine comes closest but doesn't cover all of it. I have used it, however, rough fit though it is. I ask readers' indulgence here and have included maps intended to show where my stretchings have taken place.

FREDERICK TURNER
Santa Fe

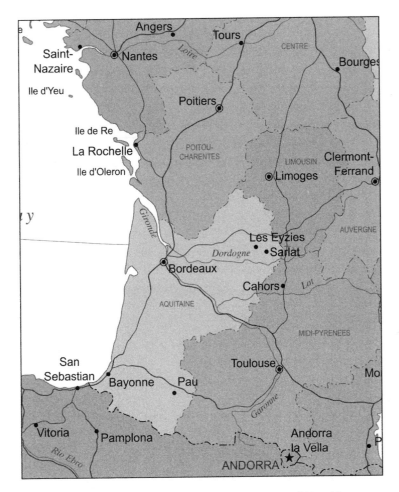

Aquitaine and adjacent portions of Tarn-et-Garonne and Haut Vienne.

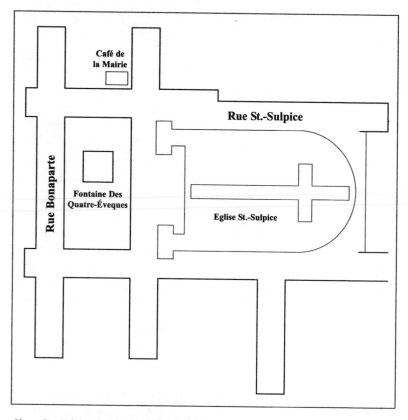

Place St.-Sulpice in Paris. Adapted from Michael Poisson, *Paris: Buildings and Monuments* (New York: Harry N. Abrams, 1999).

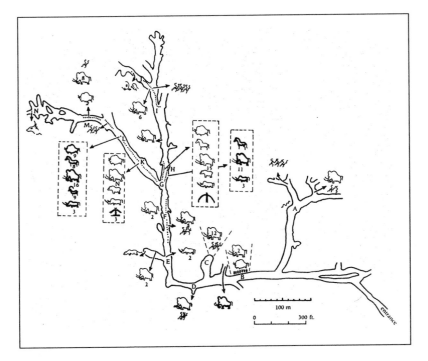

Layout of Rouffignac Cave. From Andre Leroi-Gourhan, *Treasures of Prehistoric Art* (New York: Harry N. Abrams, n.d.)

ST.-EMILION

The autumnal sun flowed over the gentle hills and their vineyards, mellow, golden as the exhalation of an ancient god whose presence here on earth had been softened by centuries of celebration followed by centuries of reverent neglect. From where we stood, the distant spire of the Église Monolithe at St.-Emilion rose up out of the vineyards like a natural feature of the landscape—as in a real sense it is: its eighth-century foundations were hewn from the ocherous limestone and chalk and up close are as dank and shaggy as a cave. Where two country lanes met in the commune of Pomerol, Alain Querre had parked his car on the grassy verge and suggested it might be good to taste some of the grapes. I followed him across the lane and into the vineyard. At this gateway to the Aquitaine region it was harvest time, that poised moment brimful of hopes and fears and memories that moved in the blood of all those who, like Alain Querre, had worked this land. The memories extended back to the quasi-legendary Roman poet and politician Ausonius, who was said to have planted the first vines here and so spread the cult of Bacchus among the rude Gauls in the late days of empire. And maybe, in ways not easily charted, the memories extended even further back, beyond the Roman conquest of Gaul, to those times before the natives learned to live in settlements and cultivate crops. Once Querre had told me he derived a profound satisfaction living and working on land his cave-dwelling ancestors had hunted over.

Days before I'd arrived here, the traditional call to harvest, the *ban de vendange*, had been issued by a member of the *Jurade*, the local wine guild, and the first pickers were in the vineyards. In years past Querre himself had issued the call and his father before him. It was, he explained to me, a call not only to the young, strong-backed workers who answered it, taking their baskets and their own individual hopes into the vineyards. It was at the same time an invocation of the spirits of the departed who had shared the dream of a perfect wine that would bring humanity's tribal factions together in love, not war. "The wine has burst from the ground like a flame," Alain Querre had called out one harvest time from St.-Emilion's Tour du Roi.

It is the living force of the earth.
It brings life to our bodies, it exalts our spirits.

The wine leaps, leaps into the air, filling it with aromas,
Bursts into empty-sounding barrels, fills up the barrels,
Steams like a volcano, a volcano of joy.

May its joy overflow and flood the world,
And fill the hearts of us all.
So that, through wine, there is no more hatred,
No more injustice, no more fear.

A noble dream this, and made no less so by the fact that in hands less loving than Alain Querre's and those of his ancestors wine was now mass-produced, here and elsewhere, like any other industrial product, liquid detergent, say, or petroleum, though at this quality level, wine wasn't as useful as these. In my own country I had seen how wine growers were gobbling up huge hunks of the northern California countryside to fill hungry vats with indifferent stuff, and I had had some menacing encounters along those valley roads with leviathan-like tankers hauling plonk to depots from which it would depart to fuel other dreams less noble than Querre's, if no less urgent.

He moved ahead of me into the vineyard now. At seventy he was still burly and energetic, moving with none of the telltale stiffness of age and with what I found an odd air of ownership: After all, he was no longer a wine grower, and these vineyards belonged to others. Still, he seemed so thoroughly at home that I gave an inward shrug and followed him down the lumpy, rose-tinted clay beds between the rows of gnarled vines, many thicker than my hand could encompass. Up close, the broad leaves were duller than they looked in their ranked masses rising up to St.-Emilion and the bell tower, some already fringed red and yellow by the steadily sharpening autumn nights. Beneath their shade hung clusters of dusty black grapes, pendulous as Time itself, pulled earthward by the same telluric forces that months before had forced them out into spring's new-made sun.

Moving down the rows, I couldn't help thinking of the first time I'd trespassed in a French vineyard to steal a taste of the ripening grapes. That had been up in Champagne many years before where I'd been on a magazine assignment. In high summer those grapes had been terrifically tart, and I'd felt a strong, silent reproof in their unready, mouth-withering flavor. Here, though, the season was right, and the grapes—merlot—were too. The first one I tasted was like a burst of sugary sunshine into the worn cavern of my mouth, which had put up with its own truckloads of plonk down through the years of my season in the sun. Why, I suddenly wondered, hadn't I paid more attention to these very telluric forces I was at this moment so conscious of, to the earth, its conformations and products? Why had I taken so many miracles for granted? Why had it taken me almost all of my allotted span to see that wine was a gift of the earth and of the artists who shaped it, that it should never be less than sacramental? Standing in the row, hand still to my mouth, I saw myself mindlessly swilling down great gouts of bourbon, tuns of beer, jugs of what we kindly called "dago red." I saw the red roofs of the mouths of others like myself—friends, lovers, casual colleagues—opened in drunken hoots and felt again the sodden agony of the hangovers of youth.

Querre remained blissfully unaware of this flashback, moving steadily before me, not so much plucking and eating as he seemed to be looking at the individual plants. Once in a while he would stop, stoop, and pull off a grape, tasting it meditatively. At last he came to a halt and gazed above the vineyards to the bell tower. Coming up to him, I asked if you could tell by tasting whether it would be a great harvest. He shook his head in the negative. "Smell," he answered. "If it is to be a truly great year, one morning you throw open your shutters, and the whole valley smells of grapes." His smile was as broad and warm as the sun on our shoulders. "Then you know."

On our way into St.-Emilion, where Querre now ran a pottery museum, we passed a group of harvesters walking along the road, their youthful faces shining with sweat and vigor and what I supposed must be a genuine enthusiasm for their work, which was no sunny saunter but damned hard stoop labor. Querre honked and gave them a cheery wave, and while I was wondering whether this special season made him sad now that he'd retired from the wine business, he seemed in part to be reading my thoughts, remarking that while wine growers as a whole ought to be natural holdouts in the age of mass production, too often they weren't. Their wines, he observed, were perfectly all right but in many instances lacked the touch of the heart and hand of the individual grower. One was often just like another. Even his sons, inheritors of the family business, had no time for the personal touch or stamp. "All very modern," he said of their practices, leaving me to fill in the unexpressed as I might.

The whole business had changed so much since he'd learned it from his father and grandfather, he went on, men-

tioning in particular the phenomenon of writing about wine:
wine reporters, wine critics, websites, newsletters, and those
increasingly ubiquitous and fulsome descriptions taped to the
shelves of wine shops, lecturing you on the various wines'
overtones of smoked leather, tobacco, goat's breath—anything
but grapes. Much of it, he thought, was actually intended to
make the average buyer feel stupid and inferior. What was it all
about? he asked rhetorically, keeping his eye on the road's narrow curves. After all, your choice in wines was fairly simple. "'I
like this girl better than that one. I'm going to go with her.'
What else is there to it but what your tongue tells you, your
nose, your senses?" Maybe then Querre felt less regret about
leaving the business than about what had happened to the
business itself, which seemed a good deal more industry these
days than art.

But he didn't drop into a dreary excursus on the decline
and fall of the wine business: He had had his own season in
the vineyards, and now he wanted to show me through his pottery museum, nestled below the limestone promontory atop
which Ausonius had laid out the first vineyards in this unhal-
lowed region and where you could still see the crumbled stone
ledges and pots of the ancient rows, the sarcophagi of
Ausonius's now nameless successors.

Once inside his Musée de la Poterie he was happy as a boy,
but a boy with an informed reverence for the artifacts he'd col-
lected through the years, at first randomly and almost accidentally: pots he'd stumbled across in rambles through the
countryside, their dulled clay sides, rims, handles poking up

through riverside mud or out of the frost heaves of the fields; some spied resting in dusty neglect next to the hearths of neighbors; some purchased from other collectors. At last, he had gathered what amounted to a kind of ceramic history of his region. And here it all was, artfully arranged in the limestone vaults that once had served another family member as a wine cellar.

He took me through it slowly. Occasionally he'd breach the boundary between the viewer's space and the installation to take out a pot and hand it to me so that I could feel its shape, move my hand along its contours, explaining to me while I held it where it fit into the region's cultural history. As he led me through the vaults the humble, ancient, ubiquitous pot, so radically utilitarian, gradually assumed its rightful stature in my eyes, and I saw it as the revolutionary thing it truly was: first artifact of humankind's arduous ascent from hand-to-mouth existence to the creation of a meager surplus that could be *stored* against an uncertain tomorrow. Coming in historical sequence after the Neanderthal choppers and scrapers, the first shaggy spear points, and then those more artfully flaked ones, here was this *container*, speaking of duration, fixed habitation, whereas the earlier artifacts had spoken of the chase, of movement, chance, and the necessity of immediate consumption. After the invention of the pot, metal-working now looked to me like a minor elaboration, for by that point in the hominid story we'd learned how to stay put, how to build villages and cities, how to herd and husband and put phalanxes into the field against each other.

TIME TRAVEL

I'd been down in this country several times before, with my wife, Elise, and once with a large and somewhat unwieldy family group. Aquitaine, of course, had been luring travelers for centuries with its seductive blend of a soft, sensuous landscape and portions that were surprisingly rugged and untamed. It was a densely layered, inexhaustible region, one that continued to repay your interest, visit after visit, as any guidebook will happily tell you. For me, there was the additional draw of Alain Querre and his wife, Sheila, whose paintings of the trees, fields, and rivers I found so evocative of nature's local moods and nuances. Elise and I cherished the memories of our visits to their seventeenth-century stone house outside Libourne. Even when it rained—as it did every single day one spring many years ago, until the Isle River behind their home rose into the lower fields, and the country roads ran like millraces.

Sitting beside Querre now as he drove out of the confusing concentricities of St.-Emilion toward Libourne, I thought he was substantially the same man who had invited us down for an annual meeting of the *Jurade* more than twenty years before. He might no longer be quite the local force he'd been when he'd operated the eight chateaux of Maison Daniel Querre, yet I thought he'd lost none of his personal force. He retained his ancestral love of the vine and still had in abundance his same bubbling enthusiasm, same inexhaustible energy, same interest in the more arcane and recondite dimensions of earthly existence. Using an American boxing metaphor I had to explain, I told him that Time hadn't laid a glove on him. He shrugged the burly shoulders that had hoisted baskets of grapes to the vats where they were transmogrified into a substance that was a blend of nature and art. Maybe yes, maybe no, his Gallic shoulder shrug said.

As for myself, riding now through the lengthening shadows of the grape-laden land, I felt changed. Time had certainly landed its blows on me. Scientific research told me that the cells of my body had turned over several times since I'd first come down here. My hair had thinned and whitened, and when I came to France I no longer hoped to recapitulate the splendid shenanigans of earlier years when Elise and I would see dawn's first smears above the glass roofs of old Les Halles in Paris or close up some smoky Left Bank *boite* with an Algerian jazz band.

Such changes in feelings and inspirations are bound to be received as shocks to a psychosomatic system that seems resolutely anti-historical, operating instead on something like that static, paradisal mode of Keats's "Ode on a Grecian Urn," where the happy boughs keep their eternal greenness and the young man races steadily in place after his immortal lover. It hadn't been too many years before when I was still privately thinking of myself as a kid. At some point, though—maybe overnight—I had stopped doing that.

But what had me feeling so different in this golden evening light wasn't so much my body as my sense that the world was a radically different place than the one I had supposed when Elise and I had first come down here. It was clearly different from the one I'd grown up in during World War II. It was different, too, from the world sustained by the massive opposing tensions of the Cold War where, despite counterintelligence intrigues and the faceless lies we'd come to accept as statecraft, you thought you knew who the enemy was. Twenty years ago Pearl Harbor remained isolated in the national consciousness as an unrepeatable aberration, and terrorism was a scarcely imaginable something happening in smoky spots so far away that to cover them, American TV networks had to rely on feeds from foreign outfits.

Now, the grim old enmities of the Cold War had collapsed, leaving in their place a shapeless, disordered landscape where no one, it seemed, understood the new rules. Pearl Harbor was no longer unrepeatable, and terrorism had come to the American mainland in both homegrown and foreign varieties. In all likelihood it was there to stay, despite the government's ham-handed efforts to guard against it. So, these exterior events matched the interior shock of finding myself an old man, and the combined effect was a kind of numbed bewilderment. How much of my life as I'd lived it had been a kind of chimera, or worse, a fool's paradise? And if the world was no longer what I had thought it was, what of my beliefs, which to some extent had arisen out of that perhaps illusory world? Were they invalidated by events that were recent but that evidently had been decades in the making? These thoughts—weltering, unsettling—formed the background of this visit to Alain Querre and Aquitaine. Except it wasn't a visit. It was far too urgent for that. It was a quest, one that had begun on a sunny September morning in 2001.

ART AND CRISIS

On September 11, 2001, my wife and I, with our younger son and his girlfriend, were waiting in Boston for a flight to Paris. We never went. Over the following few days Elise sought solace at the First Parish Church in Concord and I in the woods outside town, shuffling through a landscape that had inspired the highest moments of idealism America had ever known. On the Concord green two mornings after the attacks a small group walked in the rain around the Civil War monument, holding aloft a banner that proclaimed, WE WALK FOR ALL THOSE WHO SUFFER WAR. The morning rush-hour traffic sloshed past them, car radios tuned to descriptions of the still-unfolding events, aerials bearing the small flags that were already becoming a conspicuous feature of the national life. Two days after that, the smoke still rising from the sites in Washington and New York and Pennsylvania, we four stalled travelers rented a canoe in Concord and set out on the river under a sun as brilliant as a molten pumpkin. Just short of the Old North Bridge we heard drums and fifes and presently saw a marching corps in their Revolutionary War blood-red-and-white uniforms, moving through the tall grasses and goldenrod of the river's west bank. When they struck into the national anthem we paused on our paddles amidst the spangles of the smooth-flowing stream.

Up on the bridge itself, I talked with the park ranger on duty, a bright, fresh-faced girl, almost a Norman Rockwell advertisement for all that was best about America. She was just out of college in Iowa, it turned out, and having understandable difficulties with her duties in these first days of aftershock. Visitors to the park seemed very confused, Mindy Fimreite told me. "Some people have just stood at the Minute Man monument and just cried," she continued, "but others have been very angry. But so many of them seem utterly bewildered that anyone could hate us that much. They seem to have no historical background whatever—what's been going on in other parts of the world, what other people have been fighting about and suffering all these years." When I asked her if the Park Service had issued any emergency instructions she said it hadn't yet, but a staff meeting was scheduled for the coming Tuesday—the one-week anniversary—and she imagined that would be at the top of the agenda. Thus far, she was improvising to meet contingencies, as she had earlier this day when some visitors excitedly reported that two "Arab-looking men" were lurking about the restrooms and didn't look like they belonged there. "So, I had to go over there," Mindy Fimreite said, gesturing briefly in the direction of the facilities. "I was nervous, of course, I admit that. And there they were, all right. And what they were doing was they were *cleaning* the place—that was their *job*."

That next week Elise and I finally summoned sufficient energy and resolve to do something at last: We rented a car and took a circuitous route home to New Mexico. For reasons obscure to me at the time but perfectly obvious now I wanted to visit Monticello on our way back and then a Civil War battlefield. What I was seeking at these sites, of course, were confirmations of our essential national goodness, evidence of our high aspirations and native idealism. And where better to find these than at the home of the greatest genius this republic has yet produced, and in the memorialized fields where, as the song said, men died to make men free?

As it happened, neither site gave me what I so desperately sought. At Jefferson's plantation in the red-earthed hills I found abundant evidence of his genius, all right, his capacious mind and its plethora of interests: mastodon bones; Indian artifacts brought back by Lewis and Clark from the expedition he'd authorized; a three-handed clock he'd invented; his experimental precursor of the polygraph machine. Dumbwaiters on either side of a sitting-room fireplace could send up bottles of the French wine he'd acquired a taste for in Paris.

But beneath the sitting room, the study with its brilliant wilderness of maps and plans and gadgets, the gathered artifacts of his indefatigable intellectual curiosity, there was the kitchen. And there you encountered the stain of human bondage, hard-swept and painted up though the room now was. And just down from there, next to the smokehouse, you came to the stall where one Peter Hemings had had to raise a family, one member of which, Sally, had in all probability been the great man's mistress.

Outside the buildings, on the long earthen terrace once called Mulberry Row, site of the vanished slave cabins, I asked Elise if the whole noble experiment had been fouled from the start. But I didn't really expect an answer, and she didn't have one for me.

Farther south, in Tennessee, I stopped for gas at an Exxon station not far from Chickamauga. Outside the station door the headlines within the windows of the newspaper machines silently screamed at me: "JUSTICE WILL BE DONE" (*Atlanta Constitution*) and "THE HOUR HAS COME" (*USA Today*). What, I found myself asking the obliging man who pumped the gas and checked the tires, did he think we ought to do now?

"*Kick . . . some . . . butt,*" he grunted from his squat, each word carefully enunciated in a higher key. "Next year? When they make up the new map of the world? I want to see, 'Sea of Afghanistan' on it–nothing there but a body of empty water." Perfectly understandable, I thought, and at that moment I had nothing better to offer. I certainly had no doubt we could flatten Afghanistan, if that was what we decided upon.

Still, these manifestations of muscle, determination, and patriotism didn't give me what I was obscurely seeking down there, nor did I find it at the battlefield site where a park ranger was planting flowers outside the visitor center. The crowds had been way off, he told me, and the mood somber. Indeed, there were only five others inside the theater for the showing of a film on the battle, a decisive one. When it was over I found myself exchanging a few, distant pleasantries with a couple who'd come out of the theater with me. They were from Devon, England, touring the Civil War sites. But their minds, too, were on the attacks, and I felt almost ashamed of my relief when I saw on their faces that same stunned bewilderment my own must have been wearing. Here at least was *some* kind of confirmation, bleak though it was. "The world is a very unsafe place now, isn't it," the husband brought out at last. "Hard to imagine it could happen with so few of them to do it." Their daughter flew for British Airways, and naturally they were in anguish about her safety. "Where is it safe, really?" the wife and mother asked, looking at her husband and then away across the blazing, high-grown fields.

But that was all I was to get at Chickamauga, where the monuments placed about the woods and rolling meadows seemed silent as sphinxes, their abstract words about glory and sacrifice and duty and heroism robbed of meaning for me as if some fell foreign hand had been at work on them in the night, stealing their significance. Who were these men—many kids, really—who moldered beneath my feet in their vanished blue and gray, and what had all this death really meant? Had they believed in the glorious sacrifice of themselves, their fellows in ranks, their differently clad countrymen across the torn fields? Had they at last believed it was right to kill and to die for a cause? Or had they in that last hour—or maybe long before—come to believe that Life itself was the precious cause? Other young men in recent days had died for a cause and killed for it, too—the hijackers, I mean—and so if this was the sine qua non of nobility of soul and heroism, then maybe the dictionary of warfare needed to be revised and more narrow definitions devised.

Back home at last, I was no nearer comfort, and meeting up with friends and neighbors in Santa Fe, it was clear to me that many others were in a similar state. Each day my ignorance of the true nature of the crisis seemed to grow as I read the newspapers, watched the nightly news programs and the earnest panel discussions. As you do in shock, I picked up one thing and another, never finishing anything. I read a bit in the Koran and then in another book that told me what I wasn't getting in the Koran itself. Elise and I watched a couple of segments of a Bill Moyers video series on the Arabs. I had several lengthy trans-Atlantic phone conversations with a British filmmaker friend, just back from Pakistan, where he'd learned something of the unsuspected pit of hatred the West had dug during the years of the Cold War. I read a few of Cézanne's letters, walked in the tinder-dry woods. The autumn weather continued heartbreakingly beautiful. My study with its ranks of books and waiting desk struck me as about the most inhospitable of all the rooms in the house, bad news for a writer who ought to find comfort there if anywhere.

One day—it was February now—I read in the local paper that the Santa Fe Art Institute had opened its doors to a group of artists displaced from lower Manhattan by the attack on the towers. Through the institute's director, Diane Karp, I made arrangements to meet with them as a group. In my own shock and literary paralysis, I explained to her, I wanted to hear what they had to say about Art and crisis. What was the artist's response to such a catastrophe? What could it be? I had been living my life, I told her, in the belief that Art truly mattered in all imaginable circumstances, that it was never less than necessary, and just now I needed to hear from a group of artists uniquely qualified to speak on this subject.

Yet when I met with the nine women and men in the institute's sunny library, it quickly became apparent that for these artists, anyway, singed by their proximity to the event, it was too soon to talk on any other plane than the immediate and personal. Whatever reason Diane Karp had gathered them for, they intended to use the occasion for a kind of improvised group therapy. They exchanged anecdotes, bore witness. Some cried, others talked of recurrent dreams. One woman testified that since the attack, she'd been unable to paint anything except dismembered limbs. Another found she was placing red crosses in the centers of all her works. One man said he now wished he'd been more of an activist in the Sixties.

I came away from the meeting feeling as though I had unintentionally done some good there simply by asking Diane Karp to convene the group. But my own purposes hadn't, I thought, been particularly well served. I'd wanted them to talk about Art and crisis. They had talked instead about artists in crisis.

There had been one moment, though, that stood out in my recollections. At the time, I thought it was of anecdotal interest only, but the more I began to reflect on it, the more it began to seem resonant. One of the group, an Iranian graphic artist and sculptor, said that during the previous year he'd been in Kabul, Afghanistan, with a diplomatic delegation. While there, members of the delegation had the opportunity to tour the National Museum and see some of the damage done to its treasures in the years of Russian bombardments and then by the Taliban. If anything, the Taliban attack had been the more damaging because it was more precise. A team of them had come into the museum armed with hammers and axes, Mahmoud Hamadani told the group, destroying every work they could find that depicted living things. The Taliban, as we all knew, had also ordered the dynamiting of the two giant Buddhas in the Hindu Kush near Bamiyan. But I think this attack on the museum was news to most of us. Hamadani's delegation found the museum's floors littered with fragments of statuary and pottery. "We were trying to step around it," he told us in his soft, careful voice, "but it was very hard. There was so much of it. At one point I saw a particularly beautiful bit of statuary and picked it up. I was thinking it might be saved." But then, gazing around him at the vast wreckage of the past, he felt suddenly the hopelessness of his action and gently put the fragment back where he'd found it.

I remembered the silence in the library room when Hamadani finished his story, the looks that flashed around the long table and the collective sense they conveyed that here again, as with the towers, we were in the presence of a kind of destructiveness we neither understood nor had had any previous acquaintance with. Why had the Taliban chosen that moment to vandalize the museum when they had been in control of the country for quite a while? Why had they ordered the demolition of the giant Buddhas, an action actually carried out, it seems, by a squad of Al Qaeda? Fundamentalist Islam's hatred of idolatry was well known, but the museum's treasures and the Buddhas were clearly artifacts of the deep past, long removed from contemporary religious practices. When Hamadani and I subsequently took a slushy, late-winter walk I asked him these questions, and he had no answers. The best he could offer was that there seemed something both sadistic and panicky about the actions, as though the Taliban sensed they might not have control in Afghanistan forever and wished to destroy as much as they could while they still had power.

None of this was very comforting, and it left me about where I had been since the previous September. But one afternoon, not long after I'd had my walk with Mahmoud Hamadani, I went into my study on some vague errand and my eye chanced to fall on a kind of installation I'd created some years before. Atop a filing cabinet in a corner of the room I'd placed a wine crate from Maison Daniel Querre and atop that a scientifically exact replica of one of the Cro-Magnon skulls accidentally unearthed at Les Eyzies, Aquitaine, in 1868, when workers were laying out a railroad line. Behind the skull I'd propped a copy of the gorgeous book *The Dawn of Art*, which describes the 1994 discoveries at Chauvet Cave in the valley of the Ardèche. These discoveries not only extended the locus of the known temple caves into a new, potentially rich area, but they also doubled the age of highly accomplished Ice Age art, from Lascaux's ±16,000 to Chauvet's ±32,000.

The idea of my little installation was simple enough: that Art has a very long history, almost as long as that of fully modern humans. And not just "primitive" art, either. What better way, I'd thought, to display that heartening fact than on top of a crate given me years ago by Alain Querre, who lived in the landscape of so much of that history. For me, writing in that room, there had been a kind of existential comfort in having the installation looking over my shoulder, silently regarding my efforts to be a small part of the vast continuum of human creativity that stretched back to the Paleolithic past and beyond it, too. It seemed to assign me a place in the story, to tell me my efforts were justified, maybe even sanctified, by 100,000 years of scratchings on the face of Time.

It had been a while, though, since I had actually *looked* at my installation. Gradually, it had merged into the steadily accumulating midden of the study. But now, in this instant of entering the room, I suddenly saw it again. I mean, *really* saw it. It practically leaped out of the dusty disorder of its sur-roundings: the shelves jammed with papers, books, and pho-tographs; stones picked up in the Kansas Flint Hills, at the Steinbeck family ranch below King City, in the wheat field above Auvers-sur-Oise where Van Gogh shot himself. . . . And in that instant of re-cognition it became clear to me that my shock, bewilderment, and literary paralysis had really been a failure of vision, a failure of the imagination. I hadn't opened the lens of my mind wide enough to see the awful events of 9/11 for what they were.

They weren't after all *fundamentally* about the Taliban and Al Quaeda versus America, any more than they were fundamentally about Arab versus Jew, or the Muslim world against the godless, colonizing West. They were about all of these antagonisms, yes. But beneath them, like ancient, buried history itself, they were about the battle between the Life Force and the Destructive Impulse, its dark and immortal adversary. On that September day in 2001 the Destructive Impulse had had the upper hand, and things were terrifically out of balance—as they are every time we are in the presence of human slaughter. When you stand at Thermopylae, on the shrapnelled soil at Verdun, in the killing fields of Cambodia, the specific causes for which humans died there drift away like the smoke of old battles, and we are left with a clear vision of horror: that it should have come to *this*. Here was the real news of 9/11, news as old as those ancient skulls found at Atapuerca, Spain, bearing the telling marks of cannibalism; news so current it forms the bitter bread of our daily lives that we keep trying to digest.

I picked up the skull and scrutinized it as if at that moment my life depended on what was after all an artificial artifact. There was a great dent over the right eye behind which would have lain the man's frontal lobe, and, of course, there was no way I could determine what had caused this in the original: whether something so casual as that nineteenth-century workman's pickaxe; some shift in the earth that had damaged these ancient remains; or possibly the savage stroke of another man's axe as anger flared between two members of a species whose history here on earth is partly written in blood.

But there behind the skull was the gorgeous book, too, *The Dawn of Art*, asking to be picked up and opened at random to engravings of mammoths and horses; paintings of aurochs and rhinoceroses and bull-shouldered bison charging along the calcite-covered walls of the cave; an owl looking as freshly engraved as if finished only hours ago, not eons. And there were also the stenciled outlines of the human hands that had created all this. These productions, as astonishing in their felicity of line and anatomical knowledge as in their antiquity, were, of course, the work of those just like the people whose remains had been unearthed at Les Eyzies. And it was chilling to think—as I did with the skull in one hand and my other on the pages of the book—that if idolatry had indeed been the issue at Kabul's National Museum and in the Hindu Kush, then these productions, too, would have been demolished had they been within the Taliban's grasp. For there could be no doubt that the mammoths, bears, bison, and aurochs had been idols, worshipped in some fashion by the Cro-Magnons who traced their outlines by the flickering lights of their tallow-fueled torches.

Years before, during that rainy spring when Elise and I had visited the Querres and the Isle had bulged above its banks, we'd traveled over the Lascaux II, the painstakingly accurate reproduction of the famous cave that had been discovered in the darkest hours of World War II. Now I was positively seized by the desire to see for myself whatever works of Ice Age art were still available to the public. For this was the other half, the beautiful half, the shining half, of the human story: this primal manifestation of the Life Force, working through human hearts and brains and hands, just as the juices had worked through the vines of Pomerol and sent the buds out into the spring sun. This was what had been so crucially missing in my numbed musings on the events of 9/11, my obsession with those fireballs bursting from the towers, the official government plans in the works to exact the most terrible vengeance possible against all terrorists. I had been out of balance myself, and now I saw that.

I did not want to settle for reproductions of this art, for illustrated plates in books, no matter how gorgeous. I needed contact. Not just with the caves in France—though surely I wanted that—but with the actual earth out of which the caves had been molded and the ochre and minerals that had been important parts of their artists' supplies. I wanted to see the earth, to smell it, to feel it in my hands. Just above where I stood in the corner of my study there sat a boxed set of Thoreau's journals, and glancing up at it I thought of him, my old hero, up on the bald summit of Maine's Mt. Katahdin in 1846. He had been seeking contact up there, too, and when he found it, he knew it. *"Contact!"* he'd written of that solitary encounter. And again, *"Contact! Who* are we? *Where* are we?" In this age of ultimate weaponry, of poisons so lethal a cigar box-full could decimate a city, of almost unfettered international travel, never, I thought, had humankind been so in need of contact with its own nature and with this planet, the only home it has ever known. And surely humankind's paramount need was also very immediately my own. The answers to Thoreau's brooding, insistent questions, I thought, lay in France, in the bowels of its earth, on the walls of the caves where we have the luminous, mysterious evidence of our essential humanity and its indissoluble connections to the Life Force.

IN THE CAVE OF THE
HUNDRED MAMMOTHS

>⊷⊶○⊷⊶◁

"This actually goes better with chestnuts," Alain Querre claimed, gesturing with his plastic glass toward an industrial-sized bottle we were drinking from. Indeed, the label had a drawing of a chestnut on it, but that was all–no AOC, no chateau claiming it, no nothing. "God, I hope so!" I gasped, and he laughed. The stuff was called *bourru*, a cloudy, lemon-colored drink with a slight bead to it. We'd gotten it in the nearby village of Rouffignac where we'd stopped for picnic supplies, and Querre insisted I try some. It was a traditional drink in wine-producing regions, he explained, the first pressing of the harvest, and while sweet on the tongue was lethal in quantity and infamous for its hangover potential. We didn't have the chestnuts it went best with. Instead, we had a wedge of Cantal cheese and a round loaf of brown farmhouse bread. Even with these robust accompaniments, though, I found the *bourru* a formidable adversary, which Querre thought was funny. When I mispronounced it *"bourreau"* he laughed again and said, "Be careful: that means 'torturer.'" Too bad, I thought, I wasn't good enough in French for such word play, because *bourreau* was apt enough. I wondered whether he might be thinking that these Americans were a bit strange about wine: willing to put up with ghastly jug wines from upstate New York and Ohio and flabby, over-priced California products, yet when in France often feeling defrauded if everything didn't taste like Chateau Petrus: rather like the middle-aged male of slovenly girth and glabrous skull who privately believes himself entitled to the likes of Britney Spears or another hot-babe-of-the-month.

We sat in the dappling light of a picnic area above the town of Rouffignac, surrounded by an oak forest and only a short stroll from the entrance to Rouffignac Cave, known locally as *La Grotte des Cent Mammouths*, the Cave of the Hundred Mammoths. We were also surrounded by a busload of high-spirited grammar school kids and their keepers. They yelped, ran, hammered boulders with flint chips, gathered in clan groupings: about what children might have done 11,000 years ago when their parents were hunting hereabouts and venturing unimaginably deep into the cave we were shortly to enter.

As it turned out, the kids had already done the cave during morning hours, which was okay with me, but there were about forty adults waiting at the iron-barred entrance when the young guide rolled up from his lunch break and strode to the gate with the slightly worn air of the French *fonctionnaire*. He worked the lock, rolled up the gate, and snapped on the entrance lights—open for business. This is, of course, the kind of negative introduction you so often get at many of the Old World's most venerated cultural shrines. Still, here at the very entrance to the deep cave of the Past, it came as a shock to one who was emotionally set for a solemn encounter. I knew that Rouffignac had been opened to the public so long and was so huge that finally the owners had installed a tiny electric railway that rolled you into its heart. But the attitude of the guide and the sight of my fellow passengers casually clambering into the carts made me almost expect a call out of my Chicago boyhood when the brass-buttoned conductor would shout, "'Board!" and the locomotive would haul for the Loop. Here we hauled for mystery, the mystery of the past of humankind, that floor both physical and metaphysical where we might stand and gaze and say, "Okay, *here* is where it all begins. *This* is the place of our irreducible, unmediated origins. Now, *what* are we here?" In fact, these temple caves, in France, Spain, and Italy, are about as close to that kind of floor as we are likely ever to get. True, there are sites many times older, in Africa and the Near East. But ancient hearths and skull fragments, while enormously evocative, do not speak so eloquently of the recognizably human condition as works of the imagination do.

Yet, even as we began our journey, traveling downward through earth and Time, away from the quotidian world, I knew that we were traveling toward further mysteries. The deeper we sound, Thomas Mann once wrote, "the further down into the lower world of the past we press and probe, the more do we find that the earliest foundations of humanity, its history and culture, reveal themselves unfathomable." And so it was here at Rouffignac as our little train trundled more than a mile downward through the layers of limestone and clay, and still, as the guide was explaining through his microphone, we rolled along only the topmost level of the cave. Beneath us lay two lower layers, unplumbed, unexplored, and at the supposed bottom of which there was the black stream that had carved this cavity some seventy million years before, still running down there to its own measureless music, cutting still deeper into the earth. So that as geological fact and as metaphor, wherever we should end up on our narrow metallic track, what point it reached in the cave, we would still be in *medias res*. As were the Cro-Magnon hunters when they first came into this country and found it already occupied by the Neanderthals with whom they would have to share it for some 10,000 years.

Second by second as we clicked down over the ties a dense, dark wetness closed about us, and it grew colder by the moment as well, as if Time were winding us into our shroud. I remembered a fragment of something I'd picked up in a geology course half a century ago: that the center of the earth was molten metal. Surely, I thought, I couldn't have gotten that right because we must be close to the center of the globe by now, and it was definitely getting colder, not warmer. Or was I the odd man out? The fellow directly in front of me was wearing a t-shirt and baseball cap and seemed blissfully unaware of the crushing quality of the atmosphere, chatting amiably away with his wife.

By the time the train jerked to a stop and the guide had switched on the wall lights I was ready for just about anything, the experience was so eerie. From my readings I thought I knew pretty well what we'd be looking at here—mammoths—yet I now discovered that no amount of preparation could truly prepare you for this kind of encounter. There were two of them in profile on the wall, faint, almost indistinguishable at first from the rugged shadows cast by the lights. But then my eye picked out one of them, the engraved outline of the animal striated with long vertical scratchings as though the artist for some reason had dragged his fingers down through the soft clay. Within the outlines of the body the scratchings terminated in the underbelly and legs, suggesting the hirsute nature of the beast; and for me, shivering slightly in the wet blackness, the shaggy underparts also evoked the glacial nature of that time when the people came into this cave and the others like it spread throughout this region. Other scratchings lay outside the outlines of the body and looked very much as if they'd been made at the same time the engraving had. What, I wondered, could their function or significance have been?

The mammoth's forehead and trunk were shown by a single bold line, almost a perfect vertical, that was finally intersected by the powerful upsweep of two lines that were the tusks. Here, I thought, although there was almost limitless space to work on, there was no margin for error, since a line once made in the clay was made forever and couldn't be erased. This could only mean, then, that whoever made this engraving had done many others beforehand. He knew just what he was doing, in other words, knew how the finished work should look. He knew also how to take fullest advantage of the specific nature of that portion of the wall he'd chosen, because where he'd wanted to indicate the mammoth's eye he'd used a protruding nodule of brown flint that contrasted with the soft beige of the clay. Thus, here the cave itself provided part of the composition. In the lights that played on the figure the flint eye, shadowed toward the eyeball, appeared to be staring with a feral ferocity into the blackness beyond—or maybe it was staring down the other mammoth that faced it.

I had been wondering what my first actual encounter with this art would be like, whether it could retain any of that precious primitivism, that sense of absolute newness and awe where you are permitted just a glimpse of what something might actually be—instead of what you'd been conditioned to think it was. In those first moments when he'd seen the low, tropical greenness of the islands, Columbus had had his glimpse of the new, as it was. But since his earnest computations told him he was in another place altogether, that rare virginal vision quickly vanished behind the cloud of his assumptions, and the rest is American history. I'd seen the mock-up at Lascaux II and pondered countless plates of Paleolithic art in books, and so in an important way I had long since lost the possibility of the shock of the authentically new. But I found, looking at these mammoths, that I still had the capacity for awe. Here was no careful reconstruction of ancient art, as at Lascaux II; nor a brilliant full-color plate in a coffee table book. Here was the thing itself, as it had existed for thousands and thousands of years, before there were empires to rise and after they'd fallen, too, etched into this soft surface, a mile underground, by someone just like myself and my fellow travelers who now were listening as the young guide launched with a certain weariness into his recitation of what was known about this art—and what wasn't. And as he was quick to admit, the latter, the mystery of the art, gigantically overshadowed the former, what is known about it, like the little electric lights that were dots in the unfathomed blackness of Rouffignac.

After more than a century and a half of exploration and intense analysis we actually know little about the specifics of Ice Age art. Often our descriptive tools for it seem as crude and clumsy as if fashioned not by modern scientific investigators but instead by the hairy club-wielders of our funny papers and the popular imagination. And what little we do know is based on a mere fraction of the original whole, for the art of the caves cannot be imagined to represent all of Ice Age art. There have been found, for instance, scores of small figurines of humans and animals, indicating the existence of portable art of considerable complexity, many of these from Eastern Europe and Siberia. There must also have been decorations on hide and paintings and engravings on exterior surfaces exposed to the elements that wore them away, perhaps even within the lifetimes of their creators. Thus generalizations are not only hazardous; they are also at least partly erroneous, and a good many of these have been demolished by subsequent discoveries, most notably and recently those at Chauvet Cave.

So, the mysteries abound, and a comprehensive listing of them would be tedious. Yet it is both humbling and instructive, too, to note at least some of the major matters we don't have good answers for—and probably never will.

To begin with, the stylistic and thematic similarities of the art found in Italy, in Spain, and northward through France into Germany make it evident that we are confronted here with a genuine, coherent tradition and not the scattered improvisations of individual geniuses working, so to say, in the dark. But since there were then no permanent settlements and since we know next to nothing about trade routes, languages, and other possible forms of communication, we are at a loss to understand the large, clear similarities in styles and themes. Obviously, a tradition worthy of the term must have mechanisms of continuity, of transmission, and it must have systems of apprenticeship, for instance. How could such things develop and operate in a wild landscape but sparsely settled? How could they be maintained over millennia? Were there "schools" where apprentices learned the styles and themes, so that, as at Rouffignac, there was no hesitation in how a mammoth was to be drawn? And how could artists working on the Iberian Peninsula know much about those working on the other side of the Pyrenees; or those working along the valley of the Ardèche know the styles of those along the Dordogne? We know only that in some ways there had to be some sort of communication and cross-fertilization.

What else went on in the temple caves in addition to the work of the artists? Of the many theories advanced since the discoveries at Altamira in 1879, one of the first casualties to reflection and the application of common sense was that of "Art for Art's Sake." The notion that individual artists ventured into these difficult, dangerous recesses simply to express their creative impulses says a good deal more about us than about the phenomenon itself. Something in us finds this theory attractive, some wish to extend the modern image of the half-mad genius—Van Gogh in reindeer skins—back into the Paleolithic past. Unquestionably, the human impulse to create things of beauty was at work here—spectacularly so— but the entire context of the art, its subject matter, its positioning in the caves, the very choice of caves themselves as special sites make it obvious that the art had some sort of cultural function. What was it? Did rituals take place in front of the art as before an altar? Were these of an initiatory nature? What role did women play in them, an especially intriguing matter since it has been suggested that there was at some point an earth goddess cult among these hunters. Were some of the artists women? Were all of them? What would have been the cultural and technical relationship between the genders? One of the latest, most intriguing theories to emerge from a comparative study of European Paleolithic art with South African rock art is that the artists were shamans whose work conjured out of the rock the indwelling spirits of the animals. The psychology of shamanism has interested scholars at least since William James, and current neuropsychological research has turned up strikingly suggestive parallels between the altered states of consciousness undergone by shamans and certain images of Paleolithic art.

If the caves were ritual sanctuaries, why is the art so often very inaccessible, as it was here at Rouffignac, where it would have taken the celebrants a long time to work their ways down the long, slippery vaults to the site of the first of the images. Even supposing that during the times when the art was created there may have been other (and easier) entrances to these caves, the inaccessibility of the art is too striking to be accidental. Indeed, in some instances, as at Rouffignac, the art is not only found in the deepest recesses, it is also positioned close to vertiginous drop-offs where both artist and observer would have been in physical peril to create it and to see it, too. Moreover, the positioning of some of the art would have made it almost equally difficult for the artist to work on the chosen spot. At Bara-Bahau Cave above the town of Le Bugue, for example, you can see where the artist would have had to lie on his back to work the low-hanging ceiling with some sort of very short tool. And then he would have had no way to see where he was going with his bit of antler or bone or fire-hardened stick: his nose would almost have been touching his composition. Were there images that were never meant to be publicly viewed, that were purely private? Are these even the appropriate terms? How many images, markings, signs remain undetected even in caves like Rouffignac or Lascaux, which have been intensively investigated?

Taken together, these facts suggest that the artists often intentionally created substantial obstacles for themselves and their audiences, as if their long tradition contained within it some internally felt connection between the *what* of the art and the *where* of it, as if there was a shared belief that what was depicted was too powerful, too dangerous to be made easily accessible and so had to be placed far from the plane of the everyday earth.

This then brings up the relationship between the community and the temple caves. Throughout the Ice Age people sought shelter in caves as well as in other defensible places, such as the long, high rock terrace Alain Querre and I visited at La Roque-St.-Christophe the day before we came to Rouffignac. But as far as is known they reserved certain caves for art only and didn't even live in close proximity to them. So here again, it seems the people wanted to make their visits to these sites special events, as if they didn't wish to contaminate them with the casual detritus of daily life.

That daily detritus presents us with another puzzle because there is a striking disjunction between the kinds of animal bones found at the encampments and the kinds of animals depicted in the caves nearest them. If, say, the people were hunting aurochs and throwing their bones into their kitchen middens, why aren't aurochs the dominant subject on the walls of the cave nearest them? Why at Rouffignac is the mammoth the grandly dominant creature, when at the time the art was made the animal may already have been rare in that region? And why when the reindeer was to these people at one point about what the buffalo was to the Plains tribes of America are horses and bison far more prominently represented? Is this yet another riddling variation on what might actually be a "theme of disjunction," of some sort of careful, religious separation between the art of the caves and the life lived outside them? If it is, what are we to make of it?

These people were primarily hunters, though the slowly accumulating evidence indicates purposeful strides were being made even then along the path that led from simple foraging to gathering to designated gathering where members of the group would have been assigned specific tasks—the path that would lead to planting and harvesting and the pot. Why, then, are there relatively few scenes of the hunt? And of these few—most famously the wounded bison and the wounded man of Lascaux—there is the fiercely debated question of whether in fact these represent the hunt at all or some other situation or condition that has to do with hunting only in an associative way. Some markings on the walls have been interpreted as spears (there were yet no bows and arrows), and some scorings on the bodies of the animals as wounds. Maybe they are. But why no spear-throwers? Why no men shown stabbing the great beasts they chased and killed and ate?

Why so few humans at all in the art? And these few are of so cartoonish a character in comparison with the representation of the animals that it is hard to imagine the same people were responsible for both. At a particularly remote reach of Rouffignac, for instance, there are facing human visages roughly outlined. They look a bit like this:

—F. T.

These are goofy-looking folks, to be sure, especially when you come to them after all the majestic creatures depicted along the walls. They appear to be the sort of thing that might have been dashed off by someone just passing through—except here you are at the very back of the cave. Examples from other sites—La Madeleine, Les Combarelles, Isturitz—make it apparent that such representations are neither accidental nor the work of subsequent graffiti artists (though there is plenty of that in some of the caves and here at Rouffignac). Instead, they appear to form some part of the great tradition. But what? Might they have some esoteric clown-like function, as is seen in some of the high ceremonies of Pueblo peoples of the American Southwest, where clown figures are sacred representatives? Whatever the case, the cartoonish faces are quite distinct from those fearsome figures, the so-called "sorcerers," half-animal, half-human, that dance along the walls at Gabillou and Trois Freres.

In a good number of caves, as here with Rouffignac's "Great Ceiling," some surfaces have been worked over and over until the outlines of the animals are layered, overlapping, intersecting in a bewildering menagerie. On Rouffignac's "Great Ceiling" the clustering horses, mammoths, bison, and ibexes gave me the feeling that they were tumbling heads-over-heels from out of the sky in a sort of celestial shower. The effect was dizzying, overwhelming, as maybe it was meant to be. This clustering usage of restricted spaces has puzzled and intrigued scholars who have been trying valiantly (or vainly, as some have said) to discern method in the wild, worked-over profusion of forms. Are these actually compositions of some sort where the layers and intersections make esthetic statements, as, say, in the work of modernists like Jackson Pollock or Willem de Kooning? Or are we instead witnessing something roughly analogous to a governing theme with surrounding variations? Or, could this be something like the performance of a jazz piece where successive hands took their turns? Perhaps this isn't a composition at all, as we customarily use the term, but instead a figural language for which we haven't yet our own Champollion, who almost two hundred years ago unriddled the Egyptian hieroglyphs. One by one the major theorists of primitive thought and art—James G. Frazer, the Abbé Henri Breuil, André Leroi-Gourhan—have had their day, and one by one their often elegant intellectual constructions have proven inadequate to a comprehensive understanding of this art, whose mystery remains almost as great as its power and beauty.

And that was what was borne in upon me as I gazed at the pair of facing bison in the lights—the mystery that was everywhere in the cave, like the wet, enveloping darkness. It seemed to me in that moment of my first encounter with Ice Age art that Art—all of it—proceeds out of mystery, out of the necessitous darkness of the yet-to-be-born; out of what has not been but then, shooting through the fingers of the artist's hand, like sap through vines, becomes *is*, and so is light. The mammoths were marvelous, but so was the mystery of their making. It made me think, as I was so often to do in this land of the temple caves, of the term some of the Plains tribes of my own country used when they knew they were in the presence of the sacred. I have been using the term the Life Force. They called it the Great Mystery.

TASTING THE PAST

꩜ South of Souillac Alain Querre and I crossed a bridge over the Dordogne, the river like a black velvet ribbon beneath us and the setting sun shooting long shafts across to the opposite bank in a last, brilliant show against the encroaching dark. Ahead of us in the lowering light stood the battlements of the fourteenth-century Chateau de la Treyne, rising up out of dense woods that flowed right to the river's edge without so much as a sliver of beach. We'd been talking of Rouffignac and its mammoths, mysterious creatures, I said, whose eventual disappearance from the earth had never definitively been explained. But now, seeing the chateau ahead, I broke off this discussion of the deep past to mention that once my family and I had stayed at this chateau, which had been converted into a pricey and somewhat chilly hotel. What I remembered most from that experience was the sight of my younger son, a boy then but with the roundness of his face already metamorphosing into the harder lines of adoles-

cence, standing in the gravel courtyard of the chateau and calling up to tell me he'd made a couple of friends: two brawny
dogs who stood on either side of him wagging their tails.

But we weren't bound for the Chateau de la Treyne and
instead went by it and on into the village of Meyronne to a
hotel that was part of Alain Querre's past, not mine, where he
and Sheila had spent a happy moment in their youth. The
younger generation of the original family now operated La
Terrasse, and they gave Querre a warm welcome. An hour
thereafter, when we were seated in the dining room, Françoise
Liébus, co-owner with her chef-husband, brought us a bottle
of wine from her cellar. I'd been studying the menu, but now
I glanced up at Querre to catch a mingled look of surprise and
sadness and love on his face. He took the bottle gently in both
hands as if handling something rare and fragile. And it was
both of these, I discovered, for it was a 1959 Pomerol made by
Querre's father, Daniel Querre. He held it up toward me, its
label age-spotted and even the green of the bottle looking a bit
dimmed, but I didn't reach for it, only looked at it in silence.
Then Françoise Liébus carefully decanted it, smiled at Querre,
and went on to other tables. So, here again, was the past, shap-
ing our present moment, as it had a while back when I'd caught
sight of the Chateau de la Treyne and caught at the same
moment a heart-hurting glimpse of a boy who was now a man.

Then Querre took the first sip and smiled slightly into his
glass. "When I drink this," he said at last, "I am drinking my
father." A silence fell between us as I drank and rolled the wine
over my tongue, knowing it couldn't possibly taste to me like

it did to him. "He taught me everything he knew about wine-making," Querre said after a bit, "and much else about life as well." There was a brief, pregnant pause, and then he added, "I tried to pass something of this on to my own sons. But. . . ." The sentence went uncompleted again, as it had when he'd broached the same subject on our way to his museum in St.-Emilion.

We sat there sipping silently while the sounds from the other tables came to us in the high, stone-walled room. "I don't encourage gulping wine," Querre said then, pouring me another glass, "especially good wine. But we must not linger forever over this," gesturing with his head at the decanter. "Already it has begun to fade a little."

VENUS AND THE CASTLE

›—›—O—‹—‹

When I opened my shutters the next morning I looked out on the Dordogne. The sun was up and throwing the shaggy and indistinct shadows of the woods of the far bank onto the placid flow. Leaning on the stone sill, I breathed in wood smoke from somewhere in the village, and then, beneath that, something more, something tinged with acridness, but just that. There was a fullness to the odor that saved it from being truly acrid. It was at once ripe and filled with rich decay, too, years of it, I thought, centuries: leaves piled on leaves that had become humus; vanished vines and stalks; animal skins and skeletal remains; the powdered bones of heretics, village heroes, and suicides; discarded shoes, carriage rims, a lost ring of rusted keys. It forcefully brought to mind Rainer Maria Rilke's description of autumnal air in a letter he wrote to his wife from Paris in 1907.

He'd gone up there for the annual Salon d'Automne at the Grand Palais. But really he went for the Cézannes. Every day he went to see them and tried to describe what he felt about them in letters home. One day, returning from his daily pilgrimage, he found a package from his wife, some branches of heather she'd clipped and sent, and was moved by what he called their strong and serious smell. At no other season than autumn, he wrote her, "does the earth let itself be inhaled in one smell, the ripe earth; in a smell that is in no way inferior to the smell of the sea, bitter where it borders on taste, and more honeysweet where you feel it touching the first sounds. Containing depth within itself, darkness, something of the grave almost. . . ."

You nailed it there, Rainer, I thought, descending the steps to the now-deserted dining room where hours earlier I'd shared with Querre his homage to his father, whose spirit had been present in the bottle Françoise Liébus had so graciously brought him. That kind of feeling for the past, that sense of its *presentness*, was part of what had made me fall for France in the first place, when I saw it one summer forty years ago.

Today I would again drink deeply of the past, a prospect that was profoundly appealing but at the same time humbling and a bit daunting as well. I'd come here wanting so much from it. And here it so evidently was, all around me, large, almost unimaginably ancient, powerful, brooding. I wanted to be equal to the opportunity and wasn't certain I could be. Climbing into the passenger seat of Querre's car, I was wishing I had eyes on my fingers, eyes all over my body—a hundred eyes—so that I wouldn't miss what I felt was here, not only in the great caves, but everywhere: in the flow of the rivers, the composition of their stony cliffs, the folds of the landscape with its thick-groved declivities. Here, I felt certain, was the whole of the human story in microcosm, all the way up from the fire-blackened stones of antediluvian hearths to this morning moment with its sound of an automobile engine. I thought fleetingly of our quasi-mythological third eye, which some have identified as the pineal gland, that phylogenetically ancient organ seated at the base of the brain and which in Eastern iconography is represented as the Third Eye of Enlightenment. I could only hope my own pineal gland was winking famously now as we swung around the village church, crossed back over the Dordogne, and headed west toward Marquay. There, on opposite sides of a valley, lay two chateaux Querre thought we ought to spend some time exploring. Both had been the sites of important Paleolithic discoveries, particularly at Chateau Laussel. That had been the place where a rich cache of tools and figurines had been found in 1909, including the now-famous "Venus of Laussel," a feminine figure sculpted out of limestone and holding in one hand what has been interpreted as either a bison horn, a horn of plenty, or a crescent moon. "Who knows," Querre laughed as we turned northwestward along the Borrèze, "maybe we'll find a Venus ourselves."

The other chateau was Commarque, begun in the twelfth century. You approached it on foot down a steep, stone-strewn path through woods, eventually emerging into a swampy valley floor. And there it was, rising in ragged tiers to its high, machicolated keep. In the distance you could see Laussel. "Grim" is a word badly overworked in descriptions of medieval ruins, but it's what came handiest to me as we walked toward Commarque through rank grasses and paused to pay our entrance fees at the booth below its yellowed walls. Then we began our gradual ascent to the keep, pausing here and there to inspect the ruin's various features: grass-grown moat strewn with toppled masonry; chapel with staring, eyeless windows; shapeless heap that once was the chapel's altar.

As we climbed higher and the chateau began to close in around us I began to feel something menacing and ugly about the place. I couldn't say why it affected me this way until we came to a broken bit of wall atop which rested two fist-size lumps of densely red ochre. In the sun that now seemed almost mockingly apposite, spending its gold with sublime indifference on this monument to humanity's restless ingenuity, its vanity, its predilection for rapine and warfare, these pieces of earth pulled me back to the age of the caves and their art. Ochre had been one of the major items in the supply kit the artists had taken into the caves, the source of the rich browns and yellows of the paintings. And it was ochre that gave them that red they seemed fondest of; that they lavished on whole sections of the cave walls; that they sprinkled in skelters of dots around certain passageways and on the bodies of the painted creatures. Red ochre like the pieces I now held had also once adorned the bodies of their dead: the blood of the earth applied in hope and supplication and sympathetic imitation. And it was these lumps of ochre that now explained to me my growing misgivings as we poked through these ruins: It was the glaring contrast between that vanished Ice Age world and the one we know so well.

Often you find in accounts of "primitive" peoples remarks about their savage credulity, their cowering belief in the massive forces of the invisible world, the hideous rites they were driven to perform to appease the spirits. Such remarks make a point, to be sure, one that can't be overlooked. But neither will it do to overlook the reality of the spirit world, silently replacing it in our minds with our supposedly "rational" one, which is in fact far more fearsome than that of our hunter ancestors. In the ruins of Chateau Commarque I felt I was in the presence of a world profoundly shaped by fear.

Those who had built this pile and others like it lived daily with fear, heaped up stones against it, though they were no longer primitives in any technological sense. The spirits of the earth, of animals, rocks, trees, and caves had by the thirteenth century been mostly extirpated by the Christian thought police. The contrast was particularly striking in the case of the animals, which had become dumb and soulless brutes, not objects of worship. God was not in them nor in the caves where the spirit animals were but instead reigned in a heaven far removed from earth and from there was said to sanction acts of vile cruelty against heretics, unbelievers, and even those who practiced only slightly variant forms of the One True Faith. The world of Chateau Commarque was in fact in important respects our own. By the time the chateau was being built, humankind had made major technological advances since the end of the Ice Age, but it hadn't made corresponding spiritual ones. Indeed, it could plausibly be argued that in the great leap from hunting and gathering to agriculture and the first industries, we had simply replaced old fears with newer ones and created a model of the earth that was far less welcoming without its indwelling spirits.

Whatever you wanted to claim on that score, however, it was clear from the chateau's keep that as a cultural artifact the castle itself represented an almost imponderable improvement over the caves and burrows and holes our more remote ancestors had once inhabited. An immense advance also over the vanished huts and tent-like structures the Cro-Magnons had pieced together out of the hides and massive bones of horses, mammoths, and the megaloceros, the giant deer. The longer Querre and I stood up there in the wind and sun, looking out on the narrow valley, the more obvious the fact of that technological advance became, because everywhere we looked we could see signs of prehistoric shelters, peeping through the trees and shrubbery like old, impoverished relatives you'd almost forgotten and now might be vaguely ashamed of. Even our physical viewpoint was a gift of those who had learned how to build to such a height, permitting us our panoramic view of the past. Perhaps too the technological advances had even underwritten the profound misgivings I now was feeling, the sense that our world was in crucial ways actually a poorer one than that of the cave dwellers and hunters. Yet I could not help but feel those modern misgivings here, holding those lumps of ochre in my hands. Our reverence for the earth—our only home—had been gradually drained away like the Ice Age rivers that had dwindled to creeks as the great frozen sheaths had at last withdrawn northward. And in place of the clustering fears of ancient man, we now lived with the great fear of ourselves, of each other, of the awful weapons we had acquired. Chateau Commarque, I felt, was an early monument to this condition.

Just beneath it, I knew, was an artifact of the vanished age of myth, a temple cave. The indefatigable Abbé Breuil had discovered engravings in it that were ±12,000 years old. Apparently, the cave had yet to be fully explored, but the chief treasure discovered so far was a giant relief of a horse, a stunning work of naturalism that was testament to our ancestors' psychological suppleness as well as their artistry: They had been capable of worshipping the horse as a mythic being, maybe the messenger of the gods, while at the same time valuing it as a source of meat and sinews. True, it hadn't occurred to them that the horse might be domesticated and ridden. But they had *understood* it, in its nobility, its beauty of action, its mysterious yet undoubted connection to divinity. This was something the Greeks had felt, too, and the Scythians of whom Herodotus wrote. Not so primitive at all, I was thinking as Querre and I descended from the chateau to the valley floor and began to make our way across it.

Halfway to the far slopes on which Chateau Laussel stood out through the trees I stopped to look back at Commarque, thinking again of Rilke, as I had when this day had begun. But this time I was thinking of one of his Elegies, in which he wrote:

Who's turned us around like this,
so that whatever we do, we always have
the look of someone going away? Just as a man
on the last hill showing him his whole valley
one last time, turns, stops, and lingers—
so we live, and are forever leaving. . . .

This valley and the others of this region had, I felt, a strong claim to being the Valley of the Human Race, the place where we had most definitively and even gloriously emerged from the dimness of the unrecoverable past and into the light of history, extending from the most primitive of encampments to the caves and chiseled shelters that now lay all about where we walked, to the crumbled castle and its battlement. And there was to me at this same moment an odd feeling of vindication in reflecting that the cave beneath the castle contained art—great art, sophisticated art, art that was an older and maybe even a more radically human activity than the building of the chateau, the invention of the catapult, the cannon, the Claymore land mine.

Not that forts and weaponry weren't parts of the human story. Alas, they were too much of it. But in my backward glance across the valley I was feeling the superior antiquity of that engraved image of the great horse in the cave, its *aboriginality*, so to say, its phylogenetic primacy over the Destructive Impulse we all harbor. Surely, I thought, it meant something significant that the horse had been engraved thousands and thousands of years before the building of the chateau and the development of advanced methods of defense and aggression. And who knows? Perhaps by meditating a bit on the cave-dwellers' "primitive" vision of existence we might increase our chances of surviving the frightening technological facility that brought us the castle, the catapult, the militarization of the last blacknesses of outer space.

The valley between the chateaux was about four hundred yards across. Walking it, you could begin to appreciate what a mighty river this must have been during the Ice Age. The bordering limestone cliffs were scored and beveled to a height of at least a hundred feet above the floor, and so, even allowing for the fact that where we walked must have filled in considerably through the millennia, we were many fathoms deep as we pushed through the increasingly tangled and tough marsh grasses and interlacing briars. By now we had lost the view of Chateau Laussel high above us, weathered to the misleading cream-and-butter hues of a Maxfield Parrish fairytale illustration. As we reached a dense thicket of briars and scrub oaks we encountered the first of two small streams, all that were left of the river, and forded it, further soaking our shoes. Out in the valley we'd felt a chill wind whistling in from the east, but in here, close to the slope and where the ancient shelters were, the sun came through the interlacing leaves in shafts and spangles, warming us once more. Then there was the second stream, flowing slowly, silently in its brown bed and decked here and there with little flotillas of fallen leaves that turned and twisted, then suddenly straightened on the flow. Looking straight down into the water, I beheld the world inverted for a moment, the sun and sky beneath me, mottled by the leaves that appeared to be falling, not yet fallen–leaves that had been falling here through millennia, building the earth. And now my old hero, Thoreau, succeeded Rilke in my thoughts. Thoreau had scorned the heavenward aspirations of conventional Christianity, seeing, correctly, that they had the tendency to demean the actual earth on which humans lived. Heaven, he wrote, is under our feet, and so at this moment it was.

Querre and I had talked, in letters and phone calls over the summer, about finding some artifact of the past, another Venus maybe. And though this talk was mostly playful, we had both actually had our own separate dreams of making such a discovery–not the first time we'd found ourselves communicating in ways not easily explained.

In my dream I was walking a rural road in Aquitaine, high above a river, when my attention was drawn to something in the roadside woods–mound, barrow, some small heap of disturbed earth. On investigating this I found a partly disinterred Neanderthal skeleton, one humerus and a femur faintly daubed with red. Quite improbable, my waking mind told me, and unquestionably the residue of my background reading and photos I'd seen of burial finds in the region. But then, this entire portion of the earth, from the Iberian Peninsula northward, was honeycombed with Paleolithic sites, and it would be equally improbable that we have even discovered all the major ones, to say nothing of all the artifacts that were still scattered over the landscape.

And so, now, stooping and occasionally crawling through the thickets below Laussel, maybe it wasn't altogether implausible that we might stumble across some ancient spearhead or figurine, loosened by a recent mudslide or pumped closer and closer to the surface by excessive rains until it peeked out into the light of our time. After all, right here where we prowled, that incredibly rich trove of figurines and tools had lain undiscovered until 1909. The figurines had been grouped in a semicircle that was clearly part of a living site. Because the excavation was conducted by methods that are crude by today's scrupulous standards, it cannot be definitively determined what artifact belongs where in the stratigraphic sequence, but the bas reliefs on slabs of limestone have been dated as late Gravettian to early Solutrean. That is, ±22,000 years old.

The gem of the find was the Venus figure, still bearing along the pendulous fall of one of the breasts, in the crease of a thigh, and on the mound of the vulva the merest traces of red. There were three sister figures found with her and one male figure, but this one, looking with featureless face toward a crescent-shaped object held in her right hand, is strangely, powerfully evocative. I write "strangely" here because in comparison to the great horse just across the valley or to the ceiling at Rouffignac with its purposeful tangle of creatures, this single, seventeen-inch-high woman should not exert such a pull. Yet she does.

Is it the featureless face atop the blocky, bulbous body, the fact that while everything else is represented (even if in exaggerated measure), the face isn't? There is something deeply unsettling in representations of the human form that lack a face: Think, for instance, of the inward shiver you can get from Egyptian art where the human body may be surmounted by an animal's head or a bird's. And a featureless face seems to take us to yet another level. Something more than visual habit or artistic convention is upset here, and we sense the nearness of the uncanny, that shadowy dimension where our daylight expectations dimly perceive the shaggy outlines of impossible truth.

Or is it that the facial blankness, wedded to the feminine form, somehow evokes the numinous presence of the Life Giver, the Earth Mother, in a way that the goddess statues of classical antiquity do not? These latter are beautiful in ways we can recognize and approach, even when we know that one of their faces may be that of terrible vengeance—as it is with Artemis. Here, that kind of recognition isn't possible: the only approach is profound awe, which is compounded of fear. Enough Venuses as well as engraved vulvas have been found in other parts of the continent and eastward to suggest that these hunting peoples in all likelihood worshipped the Earth Mother, among other powers. But what is she doing in this piece of worked stone, with her left hand on her belly and her right hand holding what has most often been interpreted as an animal horn? Is she dramatizing the connection between human and animal procreation? Or maybe performing some obscure act of sympathetic magic, where like produces like, as if saying, "May the bellies of the herds be filled as mine is filled"? Or is the horn a prefiguration of the horn of plenty?

Maybe she isn't looking at the horn at all but rather is listening. Maybe she is attuned to the vibrations of the earth, her domain, the suspirations of the animals she sponsors? There is an ancient and farflung folkloric figure, the Master of the Animals, and, as the name implies, it is male. Yet it seems likely that the figure of the feminine keeper of the animals is older still. The day before, on our way back from Rouffignac, Querre and I had been discussing this, and I had said how remarkable I found it that so many of those making the recent great breakthroughs in the study of animal behavior were women: Jane Goodall, Diane Fossey, Cynthia Moss. And since we were fresh from our encounter with the hundred mammoths I thought also of Katy Payne, whose patient, empathetic, and intuitive work with African elephants had revealed that these creatures have a sophisticated, emotionally varied language that is pitched beyond human hearing and that they engage in ritual behavior that encourages group ties.

Energized by thoughts of the eternally feminine, I followed Querre through the streamside underbrush of what was for me, anyway, a suddenly sexualized landscape. The shapes of things took on that valence: the tangles of the bushes; the flow of the stream that would at last find its end in the sea, *La Mer*; the way the rocks of the cliff formed a seductive succession of V's. When Querre spotted a manmade structure ahead, carved out of the cliff, I saw it as dark and womblike. Up closer, it proved to be a dovecote, barred at its entrance, musty and dank-smelling, and evidently of great age.

Farther along we came to an open grassy field, bordered at its edge by what looked to me like larches, and then worked our way to back toward the western side of the valley where we picked up a hunters' path through marshland and small ponds. Above us the rocky woods rose out of the shadows of the marsh and the still, black waters and rotting branches, toward the sun, which was already well-spent in its shortening autumn arc. Looking up at it through the rocks and branches, I think we were both taken aback by how much of our day was done: We'd been in the valley a good deal longer than we'd realized.

There were caves all along here, high enough above the valley floor to have served as shelters after the full force of the great river had dwindled. Seeing a particularly large one with dramatically poised rocks positioned over and around it, we climbed up to it. It looked like a dolmen of the gods. When we crawled inside its mossy overhang it stank of dead, wet ashes and what might have been bat shit or human piss, or both. Yet there was none of the modern hunters' detritus you found too often in America, and I was glad of that, choosing to regard its absence as a sort of silent gesture of respect toward the huge antiquity of the place. Descending through the green afternoon light, we picked up the path once more, fainter now, and then, rounding a bend, there was Commarque in the distance, its keep still catching the lower slant of the light. Here, too, we found some of the manmade shelters and cache places, small, squared cavities, their edges only a bit smoothed by the ages.

Just beyond the first of these we came abreast a deep vertical slice in a cliff. Several veins of rock ran into it at angles, and from there the slice plunged into a tangle of vegetation. "Here it is!" I called out to Querre. He turned and looked back at me in question, and I pointed at the slice. "That's our Venus. This is the vulva of the earth, right here." Many may have thought so.

LIFE AGAINST DEATH

After spending so much of our day in what I had already begun to think of as the "Valley of Humanity," it was late afternoon when we reached our car. And since we were not far from the village of St.-Crépin, Querre wanted to pay a visit to his brother Jean who with his wife, Nicole, now ran a bed and breakfast there, Les Granges Hautes.

I'd met them years before when they were part of Maison Daniel Querre and remembered them as a handsome, stylish couple. Twice they'd hosted elaborate luncheons for us at Chateau Monbousquet, headquarters for the family wine business. When we arrived at Les Granges Hautes, though, there didn't seem to be anyone around. Finally, Jean Querre answered his brother's persistent knocking at various doors, and while we stood talking on the immaculate lawn Nicole drove up and whisked us into the kitchen for a glass of wine.

By that point in our long day my tongue was hanging out. We'd had nothing to eat or drink since leaving the hotel early that morning: nothing—no coffee, no tea, not even a crust of bread. Querre's style, I was learning, was as simple as it was demanding: if you had something important to do, you got up and did it. So when Nicole made us welcome at her kitchen table I began to harbor the secret hope that help was at hand. And presently there was a bottle of wine on the table and glasses, a basket of bread, and some cheese. The brothers quickly fell into conversation while Nicole busied herself with something, and I was glad to be allowed my silence, sipping my glass of wine and trying not to seem too hoggish as I tore off chunks of bread and put cheese to them.

Then Nicole placed three bowls in front of us filled with a rich, red-brown duck stew, the steam from them standing in the crisp air with the door opened to the late sun and the shadows of a heavy-laden apple tree whose boughs brushed the stones of the roof. Here, I thought, tasting the stew's deep flavors, was that something, that quality of everyday life, that had drawn so many like myself to this country.

After you had endured the ingrained haughtiness of this little nation, whose prominence on the world stage was nothing but a miraculously sustained feat of invincible vainglory; whose behavior in World War II was deeply stained with dishonor; whose economy was just about as large as that of California's—after you've considered this, said all this, there was still the daily phenomenon of France: this marvelous bowl of stew, this glass of wine, this basket of bread, this old house with its handhewn limestone slabs on the roof. I didn't know if anyone had ever put the whole situation better than my friend Jim Harrison, the writer and bon vivant, who was maybe even more popular in France than he was in America. "We do everything better than they do," he said to me once over a very superfluous glass of Calvados in Paris. "Except live." I was over here for an encounter with the very origins of Art, but in this casual afternoon moment in St.-Crépin I was more keenly alive than I'd ever been to the French art of everyday living. "For art to be part of our life we must live with it," the distinguished American architect Benjamin C. Thompson once observed. "In a way, things like museums and Lincoln Center kill art and music. Art is *not* for particular people but should be in everything you do—in cooking, and, God knows, in the bread on the table, in the way everything is *done.*"

When we'd finished our meal, Jean wanted to show me through the main house, both its guest rooms and the family ones as well. The former were sparkling, attractive, and simply arranged, but what drew my attention was a long, spare room—a hall almost—furnished only with mats. This was a place of meditation, Jean explained, and I gathered he and Nicole had begun some sort of group that met regularly here. On the walls of the room were photos of spiritual leaders, including one of the late Bhagwan Shree Rajneesh. And there was here as well the photograph of a beautiful young woman, the same young woman whose photo I'd noted in another room. When we'd completed our tour and Alain Querre and I had a moment together under the apple tree outside the kitchen I asked him about her. Was she a daughter perhaps?

He sighed deeply and looked off across the rolling meadows beyond the lawn. "Yes, she was their daughter," he said slowly, choosing his words. "She was living in Paris. Some men followed her home, forced their way into her apartment, and raped her. But they were not satisfied with that because then they threw her out of the window to her death. It has all been the most unimaginable tragedy for them. And now it begins again." He explained that because of legal technicalities there remained questions about the rights of the defendants, and so further proceedings were scheduled, further court appearances for the stricken parents. They would be forced to undergo the sickening event again, like the dreamer who helplessly revisits his trauma in a recurring nightmare.

Several times since our arrival at Les Granges Hautes it had crossed my mind that Jean and Nicole had seemed burdened with something. They were, of course, considerably older than when we'd first met—and so was I. But, it wasn't, I'd been feeling, a matter so much of age, which physically they both seemed to bear well. It was a something else I felt coming from them, despite their generous, spontaneous hospitality. And now I had it. I almost wished I hadn't.

Almost. But there was, I thought, something of value to be learned here in the quiet drama at this country bed and breakfast: The father and mother were trying—valiantly, it seemed to me—to get on with their lives. The entire operation of Les Granges Hautes was beautifully done, down to the small details.

The meal that Nicole had just served us was a simple, thoughtful work of art. And they had created a meditation seat where their neighbors might come to open themselves to the healing silence. I had to see a sort of triumph in this effort, the Life Force expressing itself through these people and surmounting the Destructive Impulse that had expressed itself through the men who had forced their way into a Paris apartment to do their worst. I was trying to articulate something of this to Alain Querre when his brother came out of the house to join us.

He was wondering, Jean Querre said to his brother, whether we might be up for a bit more adventure in what remained of the daylight. If so, he would lead us to a haunted chateau, though he was too busy just now with guests to explore it with us. Alain knew Chateau Paluel but hadn't visited it in many years and couldn't remember the way. "You must see it, Fred," he said with characteristic enthusiasm. "The fountain there, the 'Four Rivers of Paradise,' is really worth the effort."

By the time we arrived at a spot on a country lane not far from St.-Crépin the light was going fast. No structure was visible from where we parked, only the bordering banks along the roadbed that indicated by their height the great age of the road itself. It was too winding, I thought, to have been laid out by the Romans, who liked their ways straight, but it might have been even older than the Roman ones. The banks were covered in thick, tangled vegetation, some of which looked suspiciously like poison ivy, but I said nothing as Jean Querre instructed his brother in the secret back way into the chateau.

Then we shook hands, and Jean was gone, back to his duties, to Nicole, to his grief.

All I knew of Chateau Paluel was what the brothers had told me: that it was a long-abandoned thirteenth-century ruin that had in what had once been its formal garden a marvelous fountain that was still intact. It lay somewhere up the slope behind one of the banks, and Jean had said there was a tunnel up there by means of which you could gain access to the chateau's interior. Up we climbed, hand over hand, clinging to roots and overhanging branches, Querre leading the way. He looked agile as a stripling, though considerably broader in the beam, and so I thought again of how gently Time was handling him—or maybe it was that he moved too fast, too constantly for Time to close in. He was evidently following a path of some sort, but it had to be mostly a memory trace because I couldn't see much in the way of markers, except here and there a worn patch of dirt. Certainly nobody had been up this way very recently.

Then the gloom of the slope grew more concentrated, and ahead of us rose the walls of the chateau—huge, shapeless from this angle and in this light, covered with the veins of the plant life that had invaded it in its long neglect. There was the tunnel entrance as well, a low, squared hole looking a bit like a fireplace. We went in on hands and knees, crawling gingerly along in what was instantly almost total darkness. We'd gone about five minutes in this fashion when Querre said he'd reached a wall. There was a hole in it, he told me, and I could hear him pushing himself through it, his breath short and punctuated with effort. Then it was my turn, and I found myself unable to squeeze through the broken masonry. "Well, *shit!*" I muttered. Querre was a good deal broader than I, but somehow he had managed what I couldn't. I tried it again from a different angle, sideways, my head and one shoulder first, and found I could make it, though there was a slight rending sound from somewhere about my clothing.

On the other side I could stand upright and followed the faint sound of Querre's footsteps through the rubble and the furry dust, my hands feeling for either side of the shaft. Ahead there was a dim grayness that grew steadily stronger until we had arrived at the bottom of what we could see was a narrow, spiral staircase. At its top we emerged into a vaulted chamber perhaps fifty feet long and twenty high. This was the main hall, at one end of which were the remains of what had clearly been a superbly ornate fireplace and mantel. As we stood there in the wan, watery light making its way through jagged holes that had been windows, Querre explained that the chateau had been long abandoned when it had been taken over by the *maquisards*, the rural bands of Resistance fighters at the beginning of the war, and used as a meeting place and storage facility during the Occupation. Then the Nazis had discovered it, no doubt, he said, with the assistance of *collaborateurs*, and had driven the *maquis* out, appropriating a portion of it as a regional garrison. At the end of the Occupation, with the Nazi forces reduced by the shifting tides of war, the *maquis* had firebombed the building, killing the commandant and many others.

There were no easily detectable signs of this last episode. There was so much destruction all around: the slow, casual, inevitable work of decay, gravity, and other natural forces, the equally casual, serial work of vandals, that you couldn't tell what damage had been done when. There were smashed bottles everywhere, especially near the fireplace, as if vandals had been enacting a sort of Black Sabbath version of the highborn habit of throwing crystal goblets into the flames. There were rock band allegiances spray-painted on available surfaces and a slogan alleging membership in the Mexican mafia. And everywhere in the still air of evening was the ammoniate smell of piss. Outside the hall on the high walls were long reaches of smoke stains, but it was impossible to say whether these were the residue of the *maquis's* final, retaliatory raid. I kind of hoped they were. And there was another portion of the ruin that had housed the family tombs. You could still make out portions of a few of the inscriptions, but the crypts had long since been broken open by grave robbers, smashed by vandals, their lids reduced to slanting shards.

While I was regarding this wasteland of old pride and position, Querre was outside, casting about for the fountain that had been the chief reason for our visit. He couldn't locate it anywhere and was puzzled: He remembered it as right outside the tombs. While he looked about for bearings I stepped to the edge of what I supposed had been a ledge of the formal garden. Thirty feet below me in the last of the swimming light sat a broad pedestal surmounted by nothing. I called Querre over, asking whether that might have been it. He was dumbfounded. A long moment passed before he said that thieves had somehow found the means to make off with the sculpture of the Four Rivers of Paradise. How they could have gotten block, tackle, and truck in here by another entrance he couldn't imagine, but the theft couldn't have been managed otherwise.

"Gone," he said, his hand to his chin in wonder, looking down through the gloom at the truncated and now useless mass of stone that had once been beautiful, shedding its silent joy on generations of beholders. "Gone." He gave a shrug, and his hands rose slightly in an eloquent, ambiguous gesture.

BALANCE

By arrangement Querre and I met up with Daniel Monnier and Claude Fournié at the hamlet of Bouziès, just below the picture-postcard village of St.-Cirq-Lapopie. We found them having coffee at a streetside café in a brilliant sun that had emerged out of the chilly white fog in which we'd left Meyronne, driving due south toward Cahors. Fournié was a custom woodworker, Monnier a sculptor, and it was his work we'd come to see. Querre saw it as a continuation of the great tradition of the ancient artists who'd worked the natural surfaces of Aquitaine. Monnier hadn't worked on cave walls, though, but on the vertiginous limestone cliffs above the Lot River.

He and his friend left their car in the hamlet and rode with us over to St.-Cirq-Lapopie, which was perched several hundred feet above the Lot, a strategic spot in the bad old days when it was fought over from the eighth century through the sixteenth—a fairly long stretch of civilized savagery. You wouldn't have guessed this now, of course, for it would be hard to find a more serenely beautiful place, the kind where the foreign visitor could easily imagine himself settling down for a season. From the town parking lot Monnier led us up a path to a craggy viewpoint from which we could gaze down on the red-brown tiles of the village roofs, the belfry of the church, the perpendicular plunge of the white cliffs into the profoundly blue Lot, and then the fields along the far bank, green and umber and bordered by those ordered rows of poplars I always fell for. We stood around up there while Monnier oriented Querre and me, pointing out the general location of the Pech Merle cave, a major Paleolithic site, just across the river. It was obvious he knew the terrain in intimate detail.

At sixty-one Monnier was the sort of straight-spined, unmarked man who unintentionally makes you ashamed of your habitual excesses, your sloth and indecision, kind of like the average Joe might have felt when meeting Cary Grant, who Monnier rather resembled. Whether he himself understood this effect, I couldn't say, but his company was certainly easy, and coming down from the viewpoint into the twisting, cobbled streets of town, you would never have guessed he'd created a major art work here. He seemed genuinely interested in everything we encountered on our way to lunch, as though he'd never quite seen this or that house from this approach, or noticed the carved and grimacing faces of the weather-blackened wooden corbel of a street corner shop.

At Le Gourmet Quercynois restaurant Querre took over, and shortly we had two different bottles of 2000 Cahors in front of us, and talk was beginning to flow from one topic to another. Near the end of the first bottle (dark, dense, gnarly), discussion turned to French driving habits, which the three natives agreed were quite bad, and I was asked whether America had instituted road blocks and *in situ* breath-checks for suspected drunk drivers. I said we had, but it was a hell of a big country and the forces were spread thin. I ought to have left it at that, but, emboldened by the Cahors, I didn't, of course. Steering recklessly myself now, I found myself saying that French drivers ought to be stopped, not because they were driving suspiciously, but simply because they were French. I hastened to add that I understood the impracticality of such a procedure. They let me off with a polite chuckle.

Everybody had *coq au vin*, a dish like traditional French toast (*pain perdu*: stale bread) in that it was a creative rescue of an item (old rooster) otherwise wasted. And maybe it was the wine, the company, the setting, but I thought it was delicious, and I felt I could taste the local earth in its sauce. Then, after the inevitable espressos, it was time to view Daniel Monnier's work.

A woody towpath led out of the village along a canal that merged with the Lot a mile upriver, and we followed it, the bordering stands of trees so thick in spots it was gloomy in mid-afternoon, though you could always catch glimpses of the sunlit fields on the other shore. In small meadows the grasses and flowers stood head-high, and crossing one we caught the thrilling sight of a hawk, its braking wings stretched and sun-lit, its talons flexed as it plunged like fate into the tall grasses.

Monnier saw me taking notes as we walked along and came up to me, falling in step. "With each sculpture I make," he said, peering down at my hasty scribbles, "I write a little something. Maybe, when I'm older and weaker and no longer able to work with my hands, I will try to put these stray sheets of paper together." He was altogether too pleasant for me to feel a barb in these comments on bookmaking.

Then we were there. The towpath had become a narrow walkway chiseled out of the cliff face forty feet above the river, and there Daniel Monnier had created what he now said was a "symphony of the environment, humanity, and art." I found the description entirely justified and not in the least affected. Out of the cliff's rugged veins he'd carved, beveled, and in some places polished a grandly extended composition that really did seem a symphony in stone of the life of the Lot: its flow, eddies, ripples, runs, whirlpools, snags, and spirals; its eels, fish, and birds; the whorls of shells and the stars of what looked like freshwater sand dollars. Walking along Monnier's work, I heard the music of the place in its shapes and felt it, too, as I ran my hand over its sinuous and undulant contours. On those portions of it that had been worked to a polish, the river below and even the trees of the far shore were dimly reflected in a way that reminded me of the Impressionists, though clearly Monnier was not in that tradition. Nor was he, he told me, responding to my perhaps inevitable question, really working in the tradition of the cave artists. "That is another story," he said simply. "My work is my own story. It is an attempt to create my own sort of symphony." He smiled warmly, almost as if he hadn't wanted to disappoint me in my search for continuities, standing there with one hand caressing a spiral-shaped piece and his handsome, clear-eyed face pressed against it in an unselfconscious act of love.

It had been, I gathered, not only a long act of love performed here but sometimes a lonely one as well. Through the years of it he'd often camped here on this narrow ledge and taken his showers back down the path where an icy trickle fell off a woody slope. Yet I sensed no retrospective sense of hardship or deprivation in his remarks on the conditions of his work and certainly nothing of the anchorite in his view of himself. Instead, he radiated a kind of mellow serenity within which I thought there was almost something of the Bodhisattva: that most compelling figure of the Buddhist tradition who disdains his own salvation so that he may assist others toward theirs. Monnier cheerfully looked forward to the prospect of more hardships here if he could get sufficient funding. If he could, he said he felt sure he could polish a whole section of the cliff face to an evenness that would create almost a mirror of the river and the opposite shore. That would, he thought, be another harmonizing act, which clearly was the theme of the symphony he'd created.

Throughout Monnier's discussion of his work, Claude Fournié had said little. But now as we retraced our way to the village I asked him about his work, and he modestly replied that he was a carpenter like his father before him. Had he apprenticed, perhaps, under his father? I asked. He shook his head. "Non." And for some paces that was all.

"My father was killed during the war," he said then, and that seemed to be all he wanted to say on the subject until Querre politely suggested this American would like to hear more of the story, if he cared to tell it. Fournié hardly hesitated once he'd been directly asked and indeed a quiet kind of pride now shone out of his full and bearded face.

"My father was a captain in a unit of the *maquis*," he told us. "He was what you might call a 'Socialist Idealist.' So were some of the others. Some had fought in the Spanish Civil War. But others were just freedom fighters." I asked if some had been Communists, since I knew that the Resistance had had a substantial number of them; indeed to hear the Communists tell it, the Resistance had been *all* red. And I knew also that many still believed that the movement's greatest hero and martyr, Jean Moulin, had been a Communist. Fournié said he supposed there must have been Communists in Pierre Fournié's unit, but the point he wished to make was that they all had shared a single goal, the liberation of France. And all of them—Communists, Socialists, unaffiliated freedom fighters—were wanted men. "During the Occupation," he explained, "you got money for denouncing your countrymen. In this order (he ticked it off on his fingers): One, Jews. Two, Resistance members. Three, Communists."

On a summer night scant weeks after the Allies in Normandy had breached the wall of Hitler's Fortress Europe, Pierre Fournié's unit was awaiting the parachute drop of military supplies in a meadow outside their village when they were surprised by an SS unit. The SS had been tipped by the village restauranteur, Fournié explained. "Two weeks later, they found him floating down there." He pointed to the river. The prisoners were taken to Tournon-d'Agenais (a village west of where we were) and grilled for the names and locations of other *maquis* groups in the region. But they kept their silence. Then, on July 3, the prisoners were assembled and told that two of their group would be executed as examples. Pierre Fournié, as the leader, would be one of them.

"When my father was to be shot," the son continued, his words coming slower now and with evident effort, "he turned to the (village) miller and said, 'Kiss my wife and son for me.' So, after that, whenever the miller would see me in the street, he would come up and kiss me, and as I was a small boy, I wondered why." Finishing this stark story, his eyes were bright, and of course there was nothing you could say, no adequate response to it. In a heavy silence we entered the green gloom of the towpath. Then, perhaps sensing he needed to do something to lift us out of the mood he'd created, Fournié told me that if I wished documentation on the episode, he would be happy to send it along via Querre.

On our way up to the parking lot I was thinking of the snarled history of France under the Occupation, how impossible it would always be to ever truly disentangle it and to distinguish between *collaborateurs, maquis,* and last-minute *maquis*; to identify those who had been merely passive and silent through it all, those who had looked the other way when neighbors had been gathered up and sent to the camps. And there were those, too, who had made secret denouncements and had never been detected. De Gaulle had been right, I thought, to have decided almost immediately after the Liberation never to open this can of worms. Instead, he consistently emphasized the heroism of the whole nation that, so he claimed, had struggled through those terrible years to throw off the yoke of Nazi tyranny. Two elderly Frenchmen meeting for the first time—so the proverb goes—would never ask what the other had done during the war. But that would be the first thing each would try to find out.

I wasn't over here to investigate this dark snarl, of course, and yet in a way I felt it had something to do with my quest, though at this moment I wasn't able to see what it was. I only felt it was there, somewhere in Claude Fournié's story. When we arrived at our car, however, I had a question for Daniel Monnier. What had Art to answer to a story like that? I asked. And asking this, I also had in the back of my mind the tragic story of Jean and Nicole Querre and their daughter. Monnier looked off across the Lot to the fields shining on the other side. "I do not think Art can answer that," he said at last, "at least not directly." He apparently was thinking of the visual arts here, but then he nodded at my notebook. "Maybe literature can." But he wasn't even very sure this medium had what it took, because presently he added, "If I have that kind of hope, it might be for music. Music can work on you."

I thought that might be all he was going to offer a virtual stranger on what was after all a great and complex issue, one not well-suited to conversation. But as we were taking our leave down below at Bouziès, Monnier motioned me aside.

Evidently he was unwilling to leave his response at that. If Art doesn't have anything *directly* to answer to atrocity, he said, "maybe it answers by being. By existing at all, I mean. Maybe by being what it is, it becomes a counterweight, a balance to something like the execution of Pierre Fournié."

As soon as we were on our road northward toward Meyronne and our hotel, I repeated to Querre Monnier's parting observation.

"Yes! Yes!" he exclaimed excitedly, slapping the steering wheel. "Life is all about balance. Balance and re-finding balance! Time after time! After all, each step we take creates an imbalance, which must be corrected by another step, and so on. And without the work of the artist, we shall certainly fall, all of us."

Up in my room after another fine meal at La Terrasse and lots of good wine, I found I was far from ready for bed, though it had been another long day filled with moments of great intensity. Thinking that talking with Elise about my extraordinary time on the Lot might settle me down, I telephoned her in the States, and we had the kind of long, clarifying conversation that probably can only come out of many years spent together. By the time we'd said our goodnights I felt I might be able to go to bed with some hope of sleep. But after five or six adjustments of position and bedclothes and pillow I began to suspect sleep was not in my immediate future. Maybe the wine was keeping me awake, or maybe it was my vivid memory of Daniel Monnier's sculptures, the way they appeared almost to have arisen from the river them-selves—utterly autochthonous creations where the artist was merely the medium, the human conduit. Whether this notion would be especially pleasing to the artist himself, or whether he might find it the ultimate compliment to what he'd done there, was another question.

The writers and artists and musicians I knew personally, and those I knew of like Picasso or Glenn Gould, were often enough notorious egotists, and I lay there wondering if this had always been so, or whether it was a consequence of the progressive marginalizing of the artist in modern culture. Had the anonymous artists of the caves lusted after individual recognition? Had they possibly signed their names to their works in one or another of the mysterious markings that surrounded the art? Or was their work so fully sanctioned by the group, so central to it, so sacred, that individual honors were quite beside the point? If we assume, as we now do, that the Cro-Magnons were like us in every essential psychological and anatomical way, then we must also assume they shared our hopes of reward, our fears of failure. But maybe the reward for the artist in that time came to him (or her) differently: What if you gained approbation and honor for your skill in rendering the archetypally accurate image of the horse, the auroch, or the bear, for being able to depict what all understood was the true nature of these creatures? Then your honor might be less personal, more in keeping with group values and aspirations.

I thought also of Monnier's parting remark about Art supplying a vital balance in life, just by the fact of its existence. What an extraordinary perception that was, I thought, how wide its potential application. How many artists had triumphed over adversity and even tragedy through their work and allowed others, non-artists, to do the same through what they'd created And here the individuality, the idiosyncratic genius of the artist, was not a *necessary* feature of the process, I thought. Who really cared, looking at Modigliani's work or listening to Stan Getz, that they were pretty much failures as human beings? And there was a whole largely anonymous genre—the folk blues—that had arisen to help the troubled in mind achieve a parity with circumstance, if only for a moment, while the notes hovered in the air. There, tradition, fidelity to the form, was almost everything.

Such thoughts brought me no nearer sleep, which was a bit worrisome since I knew we had another big day scheduled for tomorrow (which was in fact already today). And then I would have to contend again with the astonishing energy of my older companion, who seemed not in the least fatigued by our day. In fact, he had announced after dinner that he would be taking a stroll about the village and maybe walking across the bridge over the Dordogne. Tomorrow and its extraordinary opportunities seemed already plucking at my bedcovers, but I felt driven by thought to arise, put on a sweater against the chill and throw open the heavy shutters onto the night air.

The stillness beyond seemed absolute—no cars, no sound of a door opening and slamming shut, no music heard and then not, or a dog barking once and then again. I could see one or two yellow lights along the road beneath the hotel and sense the river, flowing black and silent. In this visual and auditory deprivation I felt a long way from home and heard again my wife's voice as we'd talked about this marvelous country, of our times in Paris, the scene of so many happy hours. Leaning on the cold sill, the image that now came to me of those Paris days was of the Jardin de Luxembourg, where we loved to picnic on a bench before the verdigrised statue of Bacchus. And always, at the end of those picnics, we'd raised a toast to the mythic god, thanking him for his splendid gift to humankind.

But Bacchus, I now thought, wasn't Dionysus. Dionysus was an older god and probably a god of beer in his original manifestation. Once in the Louvre I'd seen a mask of him wearing a crown of cereal sheaves, though his hair was represented as clusters of grapes. And there was something forbidding about that mask, its blank, staring aspect. The Bacchus of the Jardin du Luxembourg was a fat, jolly fellow with laughing maidens draped over his pudgy limbs and a bleary, vinous smile smeared across his face—perfect for picnickers who often enough left the gardens looking a good deal like him. But the mask of Dionysus was truer to the authentic mythic nature of this god who spread the cultivation of the vine from Greece all the way to India, because everywhere he went he also spread destruction, death, and dismemberment. His story is the bloodiest in all the pantheon, and the rites celebrating him may actually have sanctioned the annual killing of a boy victim who was torn limb from limb and eaten raw by wine-crazed women who represented the Maenads of the myth. Later, these rites were tamed, somewhat, and a foal was substituted for the human victim. Still, the myth remains very dark, indeed, as in that part of it where Dionysus visits Argos on his restless adventures and casts a spell over the Argive women that causes them to kill their own children and devour them raw.

What could be the meaning of all this if not that Dionysus was the mythic representation of the conflicted, paradoxical nature of existence and the crucial necessity of finding balance within it? In his myth, joy is wedded to tragedy and laughter linked with the screech of terminal agony. Life dances with death in the savage celebration of the wine god. And his gift: how paradoxical a thing it is, too. At its best, wine elevates our spirits, as Alain Querre had said in his harvest invocation from St.-Emilion's tower. It makes glad our hearts and opens them to love and to fellow-feeling. At its worst, it unbalances us, tumbles us into error and even madness, closes us off from others, and locks us within our deranged and lurching selves. Ripeness is all, King Lear says, and the winegrower might well say it with him. But this night I was wondering whether balance wasn't more crucial than ripeness, which is after all but the balance of the moment.

ORADOUR-SUR-GLANE

In the mellow late-morning sunlight Querre and I stood on the street of a village where nothing moved except a flock of sparrows flittering from one ochre-colored tree to another. Trolley tracks followed the gradual curve of the street between the stone buildings and, though no trolley had run along them in almost sixty years, they still shone brightly. Above them stretched telephone wires that had carried no sound of human voices over that same, silent span of time—no messages of daily news, expressions of sudden concern, of lingering anger or compassion. The sun threw the shadows of the buildings across the tracks, but the shadows weren't the dense blocks of darkness they ought to have been, but rather skeletal ones that traced the ribs and backbones of gaunt wrecks. The buildings had all been gutted by fires set by an SS unit on June 10, 1944. This was Oradour-sur-Glane.

Earlier that morning Alain Querre and I had re-traced the route of Nazi units that had been hurriedly ordered northward in response to the shocking news that the Allies had made a landing on the Normandy coast. And now we had come to a village that found itself in the way.

But to actually enter Oradour-sur-Glane you were forced—yes, that's the word—to at least pass through a museum. You couldn't, in other words, simply park your car, amble across a stretch of rural highway, and enter the village with your hands in your pockets, willing to be entertained by picturesque ruins from an old war. Instead, you had to descend a broad flight of steps, leaving behind you the new village of Oradour, and enter the underworld, primal darkness, where images of the Third Reich stared and strutted from the walls while maps and texts attempted to explain the finally inexplicable. You had at the very least to walk through all this, though, of course, there was no one to force you to pause and look and read and consider. After all, even if you were to ponder what the museum had on display, as Querre and I did, there was almost as much mystery as edification there.

It has been established at least that the Nazi units had been ordered north to shore up Rommel's defenses, which had been badly battered by the D-Day landings of June 1944. It is known that the Allied high command had sent coded messages to Resistance groups all along the Nazis' conjectured route, calling upon them to do their best to hold up these reinforcements—groups such as Pierre Fournié's. It is also known that officers of the Nazi units had orders to commit actions that would terrorize local populaces so that nobody would get the idea that liberation was at hand. Villagers must get the strong impression, the orders went, that the Resistance was made up of Communist outlaws whose behavior endangered the lives of their own countrymen. Hangings and other forms of summary punishment would therefore be necessary along the way wherever resistance was encountered—as it was at Tulle on June 8, where the *maquis* briefly took control of the town before the Nazis reclaimed it. The Nazis hanged ninety-nine from lampposts and telephone poles at Tulle before they ran out of rope and had to move on.

Yet all of this finally falls short of explaining Oradour-sur-Glane, a lively market village serving the agricultural hamlets around it. There was no Resistance activity here; in fact, the village was so quiet all during the Occupation it sometimes seemed the war had passed around it, as if the war had bigger things to do. On June 10, though, the war finally arrived—troops, half-tracks, motorcycles—quickly closing off all means of escape.

The men were separated from the women and children and herded into the tobacco barns. The women and children were locked inside the church at the bottom of the hill. At first, the men thought nothing would happen—some obscure security procedure, maybe—because they could plainly see their guards laughing and joking. But then the captives heard an explosion, and at this signal the machine guns opened up, mowing the captives down as a sickle does grass, one rank and then the one behind. The only survivors were the few who were buried beneath the bodies of their fellows. Then the guards heaped brush and old lumber atop the bodies and torched the barns.

The soldiers moved through the town to the church, burning as they went. There they placed an improvised incendiary bomb on the altar, played out a length of fuse, secured the doors, and struck a match. When the bomb exploded and the doors blew off they stood there, gunning down all they could see in the heavy smoke and flames.

By mid-afternoon it was over, the entire village burning, and within its walls lay six hundred forty-two dead. A teenager, tending his uncle's cows some miles from the village, remembered standing on a stream bank and noticing a bit of charred paper drifting past on the flow. It was a page of the catechism from the church. By that time the Nazi unit, the Second Waffen SS Panzer Das Reich Division, was well on its way up to Normandy and its own awful destiny.

I had known some of this story, and I knew Querre did as well, since it was he who suggested we make this pilgrimage. Still, we put in our time in the museum, looking at the exhibits, watching a film, thumbing through books on the village and its singular history. None of this prepared us for what we found within the outlying walls. We hadn't walked a block through the spectral silence when the impact hit us simultaneously. As I lurched into a byway, Querre turned the other way and looking back, I caught a glimpse of him, wiping his glasses with a handkerchief, his broad back turned away from the street. As for myself, I found I was in what must have been a *close*, or enclosure, and surrounded by destruction: topless buildings that still held up remnant chimneys like accusing fingers; indecipherable heaps of masonry slowly becoming part of the earth again;

rusted tangles of machines and household items—a wheel, a baby carriage, kettles, a car with a crushed roof. There was no relief anywhere I cast my eye. Everywhere I turned, I looked at evidence of a savagery that beggared language, that posed the most momentous of questions about the capacities of the human heart. All of this seemed to *roar* at me, whereas only a few minutes before what I had been acutely conscious of was the encompassing silence. My skull felt too tight for my brain, my breath too great for my lungs, and I stumbled back into the street, looking for Querre—for any kind of company, really—and saw him a block away, walking slowly and looking as much at his shoes as at the buildings on either side.

At that same moment, I found the village hadn't been empty, either, as I'd supposed when we'd entered it. Others like ourselves, survivors of a sort, were creeping about in the ruins. A couple emerged from another *close* on the opposite side of the street. Farther ahead, rounding the curve of the main street, there was another couple, the man leaning on the woman's arm and dragging a leg. When I came abreast of them, I found them elderly, their faces withdrawn and stricken. As we walked on toward the church we encountered a few others just like them: elderly, their faces frozen as if they'd suffered a stroke, and with eyes that stared as if blinded by lightning. It felt positively voyeuristic looking at them, and yet for some reason I felt compelled to do so.

Then I realized why: I had seen them before.

A month after 9/11 I'd gone to New York on a private mission, trying to find out what was happening, if anything, with the manuscript of a novel my agent had put in the mail the Friday before the attacks. In the weeks afterward, when I'd ask her by phone what she'd heard, she always said the same thing, Nothing. Finally, Robin Straus said, with admirable restraint, "Fred, you can't have any idea how difficult it is to do business in this city right now. *Nothing* is happening."

I had to see for myself, and quickly found everything she'd said was true. The city was a tangle of traffic with its prow now blockaded, some subway lines inoperative, taxis impossible to get, and the streets ablaze with wailing sirens and the flashing lights of cop cars and ambulances. When I called on a couple of editors I found their office buildings battened tight and security so heavy you'd have thought they were in the business of bombs, not books. Robin Straus had, of course, been right. I couldn't do any business there.

But maybe that wasn't the real reason I'd gone to New York—or, at any rate, not the whole reason—and on my last day in the city I realized I needed to go down to what was being called Ground Zero. I'd been putting it off, I now had to admit. Somehow, I got a cab in midtown, though the driver made it immediately clear he would go only as far down as Fourteenth Street. "Anywhere below that, it's impossible," he said. When he let me off, four claimants for the cab converged on it.

It was a bright, sharp day with a wind up, the air strangely spangled with sharp, shining particles as if a billion tiny blades had been shaken from the sky, and there was an odd, searching smell down here: rubber or plastic or something else

I couldn't identify. Simultaneously I began to encounter the faces I would later see on the streets of Oradour-sur-Glane: the frozen, staring faces of those who'd been down to Ground Zero and were limping back uptown, past the cops, the street vendors hawking souvenirs of the catastrophe, the shopkeepers trying somehow to conduct normal business. The faces asked questions, but almost hopelessly, I thought: *What is this awful thing? Does it have a name? How can we ever live our old lives after this?* And now, here in Oradour-sur-Glane were the faces again, asking their mute questions that had lost nothing of their agonized urgency to the years. Time and geography collapsed for me on the cobbled streets of the village, and I had once again to wonder what on earth could make an adequate response.

When we reached the church and hesitantly went in we had arrived, I felt, at another Ground Zero. I wondered whether the SS had chosen this place for a crematorium out of simple convenience, or because it was so grotesquely apposite—because they had wanted to shit in divinity's face. Or maybe the reason had been more mundane, a mere matter of some harried officer, looking at his watch and with many miles to march, simply saying, "Oh, hell, throw them in there and get to it!" Whatever it had been, the church served their purpose of the moment. Only a single person, a woman, managed to get out of it alive, crawling through the largest of the three windows behind the altar.

Those windows were still festooned with the blackened, bent strands of what would have been molten metal on that

June day, and beyond them I could see innocent clouds aloft in the blue sky of an autumn afternoon. Next to where I stood was a heavy stone tablet bolted to the wall and bearing the names of parishioners who had died in what was once called the Great War—Giroux, Gouillard, Goutteron, La Bergerie. Ragged bullet holes defaced the names of those who had, as the tablet said, come to their Father wrapped in the nation's flag. Fortunately, we were alone. I wasn't sure I could bear any more of those faces just now, and it was just as well for me that Querre was keeping pretty much to himself, inspecting other portions of the church than where I stood. But coming down the steps afterwards, we passed an old woman, supported on either side by two somewhat younger women I took to be her daughters. She looked old enough to have suffered personal loss here. She wore a veiled hat and looked only at the steps as her companions helped her mount them.

In March 1945, Charles de Gaulle paid an official visit to Oradour and said the village ought to be preserved precisely as it was so that it might serve as a vivid, continuing reminder of what had been done here and elsewhere. The year following, the National Assembly designated the place a historic monument. At the time, the intent had been twofold: to honor the victims of this atrocity, and to be a symbol of all the Nazi atrocities. Gradually, though, while the specific horror of Oradour-sur-Glane didn't fade, the significance of the site began to broaden like a spreading stain and came to include not only Germany's sins but the greater, international one of genocide, which the Nazis hardly invented and which now has actually become numbingly commonplace in our time, as in Rwanda and Bosnia.

Meanwhile, the ruins here have continued to weather away, the buildings to crumble, the black shadows of fire to be bleached by rain and snow and what the French call *Le Beau Soleil* (the good sun) that peeled away the scabs of murder. Nature itself seemed to want to forget, to want humans to forget. And there were some in the new village built adjacent to the old one who thought it might be best to let Nature take its course. Some in the new village felt that the ruins cast a long and baleful shadow over their valiant efforts to begin life anew. Others felt there was something ghoulish in "living off the dead" by turning the ruins into a tourist attraction. Still, in order for the village to fulfill its memorial mission, the ruins would have to be preserved, artificially, and so in recent years careful restoration work had been done to stabilize the buildings. Little could be done, though, to prevent the bleaching and rusting. Here as everywhere else on the planet the present and its forces ceaselessly gnawed away at the past in both its sublime and its terrible aspects.

Walking back to the car, Querre and I said almost nothing. Finally, however, I said, "Well, Alain, the poor old cavemen couldn't have imagined doing this, I don't think." "Oh, no, no, no," he came back softly. "This is intelligence with the addition of malice." We walked past a bright street of the new village where people sat under awnings having a meal, and so I asked if he wanted a cup of tea or a glass of wine. "Not here," he muttered. "They must live here, but. . . ." And we walked on.

I wondered how life could be conducted in plain view of the ruins, whether after a while you didn't really see them any longer. Or whether, after you'd ceased to see them, they might come back to you some night, full-force, like a revenant, and you'd wake locked in icy horror. I wondered, too, whether it would be better after all to let Nature take its course until at last nothing would be left but a few gentle mounds of stone, like the ruins at Glastonbury, England, the supposed seat of Arthur's kingdom. There was something in this image that was comforting when I put it together in my mind with the temple caves. For if these ruins did finally topple into the patient, waiting earth, then the contrast between the Life Force and the Destructive Impulse might be even more impressive than it was now. True enough, had the art of the caves been exposed as were the ruins at Oradour-sur-Glane, we could never have imagined its splendid existence. But it wasn't. It was carefully sheltered by people who knew a great deal more about the effects of weather than almost anyone alive today. It was sheltered, in part at least, because those people *wanted it to endure*: to endure as testaments to their collective engagement with the Infinite, the Life Force, the Great Mystery—the names mean so little, even less when you consider what has been done because of them.

Directly across the road from the parking lot an old white horse and a small brown donkey stood side by side, looking over a barbed wire fence. Behind them ran the wall of the old village and beyond that the ruins, shadowed by oaks. I couldn't tell what the animals were thinking, but it was obvious that they were sharing the moment and its peace. I stopped to take a photo of them. They were different animals, but they had learned how to get along.

DREAM OF THE MYTHIC PAST

⊱━◆━◯━◆━⊰

When Alain Querre told me he must get back to his life with Sheila in Libourne and to his museum in St.-Emilion, I rode back with him to pick up a car at the Libourne train station. The morning following I met the early train from Paris. My old friend, Guy de la Valdene, had said he'd like to come down from his Normandy home for *un petit tour gastronomique* (a little eating tour) of restaurants in Aquitaine and wouldn't mind seeing a couple of the caves between meals. I waited for him on the crowded platform as the long train disgorged its passengers, and just as I'd begun to think he'd missed it, here he came, emerging from the stairwell, huffing, red-faced, and dragging a large bag. It had been, he presently explained, a big night in Paris where he'd stopped over with friends.

Guy was built along classic Norman lines: big-boned, broad-shouldered, handsome in that rough-hewn northern way. He was most at home in the fields with his dogs and gun or in his kitchen, sweating over his top-of-the-line stove. He was also a writer and a good one, I thought, but except on rare occasions it was difficult to get him to talk about that. There was a deep diffidence there, and I didn't know where it came from: whether it was modesty, shyness, or a reluctance to discuss with anybody matters of so personal a nature. You find writers and painters like this once in a while, and when you do it can be something of a disappointment, unless they have other interests that serve as beguiling substitutes for talk about their art. Guy did. He was bluff, funny, marvelously profane, and he knew good food and wine.

Walking across the lot from the station, I noticed him scanning the cars with more than casual interest. "This is it," I told him as we reached a silver four-door Mercedes. "I reserved a two-door Opel, but this was all they had left." He laughed, heaving his bag into the back seat.

"I was afraid you'd have some little *boite de merde* (shitbox) for us," he said, "and my fucking *knees* would be up against the dash all day. I know you'd never *order* something like this."

The car was a good one and Guy an accomplished map-reader, and we spent the day in a leisurely meander through the *bastides* (fortified towns) for which the region was famous, heading southeast to Puymirol where there was a hotel with a three-star restaurant he wanted to experience. The dinner was on him, he reminded me. By the time we arrived, hauling up the narrow traverses of the thirteenth-century town built by one of the counts of Toulouse, the sun was well spent and shooting long fingers down the main street. What few shops

there were had been shuttered up, and about the only signs of
life were the youngsters in starchy livery you could see going in
and out of L'Aubergade, the hotel, which shortly proved lux-
urious enough to suitably house a three-star restaurant.

Guy had already complained about having to lug coats and
ties down here for our dinners. They definitely were not his
customary wear; in fact, the only other time I'd seen him
dressed up had been years before in Paris when he'd hosted Jim
Harrison and me at the Taillevent. So now, at our table on the
heated terrace, he was tugging at his shirt collar and swearing
under his breath. It was loud enough, however, to cause our
near neighbors to glance over, but then the place lay under a
deep hush.

There is a level of French dining that is so elegant and rar-
ified it unintentionally tumbles over into the silly. You know
you've reached it when you feel like you've blundered into a
mortuary instead of a place of enjoyment, and there are as
many flunkies flitting about as there are diners. This was one of
those places, and indeed, as it turned out, everything about the
experience was on the silly side. The wine list was a little thicker than the Winnetka telephone directory, and I was glad to let
Guy have a crack at it while the sommelier hovered, rubbing his
hands with the unctuousness of a funeral director about to
describe the available services. When the young man had
departed to fetch our bottle Guy dryly observed that his selection was so expensive we would have to truly savor it, otherwise
it wouldn't last us through dinner. As it happened, his concern
was unfounded. The wine was expensive, all right, but it arrived
with dinner, and the sommelier made such a production of

serving it I was beginning to hope it went well with dessert. He rolled the bottle between his palms; he decanted it; he sniffed the cork and then the wine itself; he poured himself a thimbleful and sniffed that. And then he didn't pour for us but went off on some other mission, leaving the decanter sitting there on the serving table and definitely out of reach. I had seen Guy give decorum a swift kick in the scrotum on other occasions, and it amused me to find that here he was able to restrain himself until the sommelier returned for the main event. At just about the same moment the chef appeared among the tables, gauging the clientele's reactions to his art. He was dressed like a cross between a pirate and a beachcomber.

The next morning, though, all was forgiven. The weather was holding beautifully, and ahead of us we had the experience of the great Pech Merle Cave. Our route took us up through more of the *bastides*–Bourg-de-Visa, Lauzerte, Montcuq–and through the city of Cahors. And since it was a Saturday, all along our way we saw the weekend outdoor markets, a French phenomenon I have always found so appealing. The local products, all fresh, all home-grown or -raised, or -slaughtered, were out there for the expert scrutiny of the housewives and husbands who not only knew these products but who had brought them there to market. Some of my best moments in this country–right up there with museums, an authentic bistro meal, and Daniel Roth on the famous organ at St.-Sulpice church in Paris–have been spent at these outdoor markets, which are truly spectacles as well: in St.-Rémy, Provence, where the bins of spices almost blinded you with the unadulterated colors of the sun-drenched soil; at St.-Pierre-sur-Dives,

Normandy, where one raw autumn morning I counted four-teen different varieties of sausage; and at Place Maubert, Paris, where the vegetable vendor rang his high chant, *"Dix francs! Dix francs!"* over the meditative crowd of shoppers. Passing through the hilltop towns, we caught glimpses of the awnings of the markets and saw shoppers trundling carefully downhill with wicker baskets looped over arms and bulging plastic sacks hanging from both hands. We were tempted to stop and would have, surely; but we had the grand cave awaiting us like some darkly luminous lodestone.

It was market day in Cahors as well, and the city was properly congested, but we worked our way through to the other side and followed the Lot up to Pech Merle outside the village of Cabrerets.

Pech Merle was part of a large complex of caves—over a hundred of them—that were once inhabited. A dozen of the caves were decorated, principally Cougnac with its depictions of the great-horned deer, the megaloceros. But Pech Merle with its Black Fresco and the Panel of the Dotted Horses is one of the major Paleolithic sites in the region, the object of intense scholarly scrutiny since its discovery in 1922.

We went in with a crowd of American college kids who were spending their junior year abroad. There was the normal amount of giggling and undisguised verbal foreplay while we waited to be guided through the doorway and down the clammy steps, but once we were down on the floor of the cave the magic of the place took hold, and the kids were respectful, maybe even awed. It would have been hard not to be, for the cave's natural formations were in themselves so spectacular they bordered on the Disneyesque. The calcite had coated the stalagmites and stalactites with a shiny patina that, in the dramatic lighting, made them look unreal. The first impact was a bit like the kind of kitsch you might find in Ohio or Kentucky where Gert and Randy had a cavern on their property and had tricked it out like a creepy-crawly fun house.

But then you got to the art, and once you caught your first sight of it, the shining formations and dramatic lights dropped away and your skin bristled in the presence of the luminous mystery: work done by hands just like ours ±18,000 years ago. The Black Fresco dominated the decorated portion of the cave. It was a worked and reworked panel of oxen, horses, mammoths, bison, and signs. Intermingled were conjectured spears, wounds, animal breath and blood, all of it outlined in black manganese. I found the mammoths particularly stunning in their free felicity of line and scribbled something to that effect in my notebook; looking at the page later that day, the note seemed silly simply because *all* the figures were so beautifully rendered with that seeming effortlessness that so often is the sign of high art.

The more I looked at the figures, the more I thought I saw a stylistic resemblance to classic Chinese calligraphy where the artist guided the brush with a flowing, continuous motion from first stroke to last, and where, as Alan Watts wrote, to hesitate was as fatal as to hurry. In the hands of a master calligrapher, Watts explained, the brush seemed to be writing on its own, like a river following the natural contours it has itself made. "The beauty of Chinese calligraphy," he wrote, "is thus the same beauty which we recognize in moving water, in foam, spray, eddies, and waves, as well as in clouds, flames, and the weavings of smoke in sunlight." The Chinese call this special beauty the following of *Li*, Watts said, which means following the organic pattern of all things, and in order to achieve this level of mastery, you had to undergo an extensive period of apprenticeship. The same must have been true, it seemed to me, of the Ice Age artists, for although there is in all the known examples of the art no suggestion anywhere of the natural contours of nature, no least hint of landscape or waters or indeed anything except the animals themselves, still these artists followed the contours of the animal bodies with a scrupulous fidelity and lean felicity that could only come from some system of apprenticeship. How else could the great tradition have been maintained over millennia if not through such a system? For, whereas its meanings will always be in doubt, its antiquity and its continuity are not. It fully justifies André Leroi-Gourhan's characterization of it as the "longest and oldest of the artistic adventures of mankind."

When Leroi-Gourhan wrote those words Chauvet Cave had yet to be discovered, and since the art found there was as fully accomplished as the best of Lascaux or Pech Merle, the shadowy foreground in which the tradition took shape and a system of apprenticeship developed must extend yet further back in time, back beyond the advent of the Cro-Magnons into Europe—all the way back to Africa, it seems. The evidence from the Blombos Cave in South Africa, where decorated objects have been dated ±70,000 years old, strongly suggests that Art and modern humanity may be coeval. As Randall White, the American expert on Ice Age art, put it, the great antiquity of Art must mean that it "conferred upon humans some considerable evolutionary and adaptive advantages." Put another way, we wouldn't be the species we have become without Art.

Whatever discoveries await those working with the sites already known, and those other patient adventurers searching for "new" sites, their faces pressed close to the rocks in hopes of feeling the earth's breath from some deep cavity below, whatever new depths are to be sounded in the search for the bottom flooring of humankind's unfathomed past, Pech Merle's Black Fresco will do beautifully as the classic illustration of the fully mature Ice Age art. Close analysis of it has revealed a good deal about the technical workings of the great tradition.

The outlines of the animals in the fresco were first sketched in by the artist, using some sharp-pointed object, whether stick or bone or antler fragment. Then the master began to trace with manganese the mammoths, bison, and others of the running, tumbling menagerie. He used four long, sinuous strokes to evoke a mammoth. Nine for an auroch. Eight made a horse appear out of the wall, thirty a bison—shaggy, big-shouldered, dense. Such analysis confirms the hypothesis of apprenticeship whereby the artist's hand and arm were being guided by a knowledge of the way it was done, the way it had always been done. Perhaps almost as remarkable as this knowing economy of line and the relationship of line to mass is the experts' conclusion that the Black Fresco was the work of a single artist who executed all of it in one long, sweeping session. And this is the more remarkable yet when you reminded yourself that the electric lights in which you beheld the fresco were unavailable to him, and he worked instead by the inconstant, guttering flare of tallow-fueled torches and lamps. This could only mean, of course, that the light he really worked by was inner, that it came to him out of the long, echoing past.

Leroi-Gourhan has tried to read this fresco (as well as the other large panels of parietal art) as if it were a composition in a pictorial language that was probably esoteric even in those times. I think he was right to do so, though his elegant, uniquely French, intellectual edifice seems finally not to explain very much—as the great scholar himself humbly admitted in his masterwork *Treasures of Prehistoric Art*. This is a visual language we don't have the key for, he said there, and probably never will. We have a rough chronology for the art based on stratigraphic evidence. We have enough examples of it to posit the existence of a great tradition extending over thousands of years. And the evidence from the caves tells us of the materials the artists worked with and something of their working conditions. From a few calcified footprints (including one in Pech Merle) we know that children and young adults were in the temple caves, which scanty evidence has led some to posit that the art in its characteristically inaccessible settings functioned as the setting for initiation rites. But we know nothing of what sort of rites these might have been or how the art figured in them.

The fox knows many things, but the hedgehog knows one big thing, Archilochus famously, and enigmatically, wrote. And we know one big thing, too. We know that here in Pech Merle and in the other temple caves we are in the presence of a mythology. We may always lack the key to reading the sacred narratives that run along the ceilings and walls, but we know they were narratives of some sort in which the animals stood in a special relationship to the Powers, were perhaps their earthly emissaries. And we know that the art—all of it—comes out of a period in the mental history of hominids when everything appeared to exist in that harmonious, undifferentiated state of balance that every mythology gestures back toward but which, perhaps, no peoples ever actually witnessed. "In the very earliest time," went an Eskimo song,

> *When both people and animals lived on earth,*
> *a person could become an animal if he wanted to*
> *and an animal could become a human being.*
> *Sometimes they were people*
> *and sometimes animals*
> *and there was no difference.*
> *All spoke the same language.*

Even if this magical interchangeability, this undifferentiated state of balance, was a thing of the past 18,000 years ago (or was, as many would have it, a purely imaginary state), these drawings and paintings take us back close to it. They allow us to experience it imaginatively. And *that* may be their inexhaustible utility for us. They tell us—they *show* us—that the modern human story begins with the blood-and-bone understanding that Life is One. That the same force that flung clus-

ters of crystals into the darkest recesses of the caves in profligate profusion is the very same force that grew the grasses
upon which the great herds and their human predators
depended. This art *reminds* us how interconnected everything
was and still is, as when the creatures' outlines intersect and
they tumble over each other like a galaxy of heavenly bodies,
and humans have horns and tails and join in the dance. It
shows us, too, that *everything* on earth is ultimately sacred, as
when an entire portion of a cave was slathered with red ochre.
It shows us, finally, that Life feeds on Death in a sacred balance that must be respected so that it may be sustained. When
we truly come into the presence of this art, open to what it has
to tell us in an unknown tongue, we know these perceptions
are *not* modern impositions in which cavemen are made over
into ecumenical ecologists. They are not the gauzy maunder-
ings of flower children or bunny-huggers. They are the oldest
and the truest perceptions about existence we have ever had,
ever will have. And this ancient art is perhaps the most direct
way we have left to make contact with these timeless truths in
our own, unbalanced, epoch.

From an immediate, technical point of view, what made
the ancient art possible was the human hand, its dexterous
thumb-and-forefinger opposition, the breadth of the end
bones of the fingers, the long thumb, the strong, flexible muscles webbing the thumb to the first two digits. And it was to
the artistic evidence of this evolutionary phenomenon that
our tour of Pech Merle finally brought us: to the Panel of the
Dotted Horses and the hands outlined around them. The

horses were beauties with something archaic-looking about the arch of their necks. They were dappled with the red and black dots that have so intrigued scholars, and the lines of their underbellies exaggerated those swaggy curves. Here once again, as with the great horse of the cave beneath Chateau Commarque, I felt I was seeing the horse as itself and not as a domesticated drudge, a dumb adjunct to the human story. Art can do this for us, restoring animal, object, or everyday item to something of its original and sovereign status, as when the poet Pablo Neruda wrote odes to soap and a pair of navy blue socks.

Around the horses were the hands, outlined by the perfusion of pigment through some sort of hollowed tube, bone most likely. The juxtaposition of horses and hands inevitably reminded an American visitor of the way the Plains tribes would place a vermilioned palm print on the rumps of their horses, signifying both ownership and a pure delight in design and color. The stenciled hands here, though, probably had nothing to do with ownership. They would seem to have more to do with the human animal's sign to itself of what it most radically was. At that remote period in our story we could hardly have understood our brains, how, fabulously, they had developed and swelled so that the very shape of our skulls was forced to bulge forward to accommodate the frontal lobes, the heavy eyebrow ridge giving way to a well-nigh precipitous slope upwards to a capacious dome. No, all this would have been unavailable to our ancestors' understanding, as would the brain's workings, its obscure promptings. And so there is almost a sort of anatomical and evolutionary justice that the hand should be the sign and signature of their presence in the temple caves. It must have seemed to our ancestors that it was the hand, not the brain, that gave them something close to parity with the cave bear, the giant deer, the woolly mammoth, that gave them some unique niche in the grand order. It was the hand that made the choppers and scrapers, the knives that compensated for the lack of fangs and claws; that shaped the spear points, the barbs of the harpoons, the spear-throwers that made up for that extra set of legs they somehow hadn't been provided with. It was the hand, too, that allowed them to do what they must have realized none of their fellow creatures did: to depict the shapes of life. However we attempt to understand this fabulously sustained act of creativity, surely this is the sign we made of who we were. It's as if our ancestors were signing here, "The megaloceros has his great antlers, the bear his fangs and claws, the rhino his horn. We have hands."

At the same time, it's possible that even so early these stenciled hands might have been a symbol of a dimly sensed difference between ourselves and the other animals. The eminent microbiologist René Dubos once claimed that with small, rare exceptions human groups have probably never been in real balance with their environments. They have always been too restlessly inventive, he thought, have always understood themselves to be exceptional, have always manipulated their places of living in ways they knew no other creatures did. This might explain, then, the age-old, transcultural theme of declension, the Fall from some imagined age of harmony and balance, so poignantly expressed in Rilke's "Eighth Elegy"—"so we live, and are forever leaving"—always looking back to the happy, paradisal valley we have left behind.

Maybe this is true. But even if it is, this hardly invalidates our "memory" of that earlier paradisal state of undifferentiated grace. The persistence of the idea of this paradise and our "fall" from it means that deep within the brain of the human animal there exists some archaic memory trace of a time in our journey when we did feel in harmony with everything that was, when we were residents of that happy valley and not merely passing through it on our restless way out.

I couldn't, of course, know what the students around me were thinking when they looked at the painted horses standing back to back with their low-slung bellies and the hands outlined about them; whether they'd had enough of the cave by now and were eager to get back to the "real" world; whether the cave would even serve mainly for pillow talk that night. I was unwilling to believe, though, that in future recountings of their year abroad, Pech Merle would simply be one of the sights, ranked equally with the Ferris wheel and the Obelisk of Luxor in Paris's Place de la Concorde. I thought it far more likely that the cave would be down there, like buried history, deep in their brains, and that they would be drawing on it the rest of their lives, whether they knew it or not.

Nor could I guess its true impact on Guy. He wasn't the sort of man with whom you could easily discuss such a matter—at least he wasn't that way with me. And so what we found ourselves talking about on the terrace of a riverside restaurant below St.-Cirq-Lapopie was the culture of hunting, about which he knew a great deal and about which he had written well, most recently in a novel set in his ancestral Normandy. France, he said, had unfortunately come a hell of a long way from the world of teeming wildlife we'd just been looking at in the cave. Even up in Normandy, which in his youth had been good game country, cover had been so pruned back in the service of agriculture that the sport had been drastically affected. I knew that our mutual friend, Jim Harrison, had once been on a stag hunt up there with him, and so I said there must be some cover left. But he was into his own variation of the theme of declension from a hunter's paradise and said the poor animals had almost no place left to hide.

While we waited for our smoked duck and salads we shared a bottle of '99 Cahors. Below us the Lot ran shining between its white cliffs, and the hot sunlight through the late leaves turned them incandescent. The two-tiered terrace was filled with daytrippers on this weekend afternoon, including some healthy looking young women, suitably clad for such clement weather. We both took such pleasure in them, in the weather, and in the Cahors that I was moved to remark when we left, "Well, hell, Guy. You people have all the best of it over here—babes, wine, weather, great art. What else is there?"

"Well," he replied, laughing, "the weather can be shitty, as you know."

Le Centenaire, where we stayed that night in Les Eyzies, proved to be one of those high-end places I had no trouble avoiding when I was in France on my own—they of the Sepulchral Hush. Still, we managed to disturb the decorum of dinner when Guy began telling a story about a mutual friend better known among his cronies for his outdoor skills than his indoors etiquette. At some sort of formal reception, Guy reported, Roger was observed sniffing the uncorked and breathing wine bottles, as he'd been told true connoisseurs always did. "Except he wasn't exactly sniffing them," Guy went on, his big shoulders beginning to heave in helpless hilarity. "He was putting them way up his nose, like this." He held an imaginary bottle with both hands and pretended he was corkscrewing it up one nostril, making a snorting sound as he did so. I was glad the bottle was only imaginary because he'd ordered a '97 Carillon de L'Angelus, St.-Emilion, and it was glorious in a silky, smooth-muscled way. But just now I couldn't have drunk it anyway. Wine ought to encourage laughter, among other things, yet if you're laughing so hard your stomach hurts, you can't send anything down to it—especially not a drink this delicious. In any case, our hilarity in the plushy formality of Le Centenaire's restaurant was beginning to draw attention, despite our efforts not to turn a great laugh (one of life's supreme pleasures) into an offensive jackass bray. Presently, we were visited by the maitre d', who politely inquired if we were finding our frog's legs perfectly satisfactory. He caught us still full of laughter, so we could only sign, helplessly, that everything was dandy.

THE MARK OF THE BEAR

Les Eyzies billed itself as the "Capital of Prehistory" and with justice. North of it lay Lascaux and the immediately adjacent site of a conjectured bear cult, Régourdou, that is three times older than Lascaux. Just east were the chateaux, Commarque and Laussel, and the major art sites of Font-de-Gaume and L'Abri Cap Blanc. Northwest were Rouffignac and La Ferrassie, perhaps the single most significant Neanderthal site yet discovered. And the town itself has its own substantial claim to fame since it was here that the five skeletons were accidentally unearthed that gave the name "Cro-Magnon" to our ancestors. When I pushed open the ponderous shutters of my room on a glorious Sunday morning I looked out on the Musée National de la Préhistoire above the town's main street and above that, cut into the oak-clustered cliffs, some of the many rock shelters and lookouts that ring the town. In quite another way than Oradour-sur-Glane and a richer one, too, Les Eyzies fed off the dead whose works drew tourists year-round.

I suggested to Guy that we work along the southwesterly squiggle of the Dordogne out of Les Eyzies and just see how far we got. I wanted to end up at Bara-Bahau Cave to see its famed bison engraving, I told him, and we could easily do that no matter how leisurely the pace. As it happened, our pace was very leisurely indeed, and we didn't make Bara-Bahau until almost closing time, and yet I felt the intervening hours had been well spent: If your antennae are out, even your mistakes and meanders can give you gifts that enrich your sense of a territory in ways you appreciate only later.

We had tried vainly to find what was said to be a fine hiking trail linking the towns of Le Bugue and Limeuil, but after several false passes and dead-ends down by the river we settled for a walk around Limeuil, a *bastide* at the strategic confluence of the Dordogne and the Vézère and thus the scene of bloody struggles through the ages until it settled quietly into existence as a tourist attraction. In 1909 the indefatigable Abbé Breuil found a cache of dozens of stone plaques between here and Le Bugue, covered with engravings of horses and reindeer. For the great scholar Leroi-Gourhan and others this find seemed likely to be evidence of a "school" where younger artists learned how it was done. If so, surely there must be others, but where?

This was another as-yet-unsolved mystery, though it was at least potentially solvable by the discovery of other caches, whereas some of the deeper mysteries (like the rites, narratives, and significations of the painted animals) probably never would be. Trudging up Limeuil's steep cobbled streets to a little park, I felt once again surrounded by mystery on this warm, almost drowsy Sunday afternoon that outwardly seemed so open and available. Here we were in this picturesque little village at the foot of which picnickers sat in the shade of riverside poplars and canoeists stroked along beneath the high arches of the bridge. Had it not been so picturesque, it would have been almost prosaic in its Sabbath placidity. Yet, I felt the unknown past everywhere about. There were scattered all through this region the great caves whose deepest depths remained unsounded and those other caves that remained undiscovered, holding unknown, unimagined treasures. There were the hundreds of shelters hacked out of the limestone cliffs, and who knew anything about the quality of daily life lived in them, except for a few cartoony stereotypes of troglodytes and savage feasts of raw meat? There were the surrounding oak forests secretly sown with buried spear points and millions of flint flakings. And maybe there were other yet-to-be discovered female figurines stashed in stray crevasses along the rivers, any one of which with its markings might speak to us in still more certain terms of the cult of the Earth Goddess.

Even the smell of the streets we followed to the hilltop park had a quality of mystery about it. I couldn't identify it except to sense that it was a compound of great age, something musty, slightly dank about its edges, *settled*. The streets were lined on both sides with gutters that had carried loads of human and animal waste down to the river and, given the town's strategic location, had doubtless run with blood in their time. When we came across an old man sitting on a low stone wall with his walking stick and Brittany spaniel, I wondered what he'd seen in a long life that was near its close, what he knew of the war and the Occupation, and I knew for certain only that I would never know. *That*, surely, was one of the great mysteries we daily lived with: the unknowable lives of others.

The hilltop park had an old *pigeonnier* near one edge of it and an *allée* of chestnut trees along another, and walking along through the *allée*'s ordered bars of sunlight and shadow, we heard children's voices and presently came upon a little boy and girl at play among the leaves and inspecting fallen nuts for prizes and curiosities. *"Un double! Un double!"* we heard the boy cry out as we went past.

At the end of the *allée* we had a fine view of the valley, less dramatic here without the cliffs we'd seen yesterday, but beautiful in its burnished autumnal colors, the alternation of the plowed fields with unharvested strips of corn, and the bordering lines of oaks and poplars. Directly below us was the intense green of a soccer field, and we watched from our high grandstand as the weekend heroes ran up and down in their bright uniforms with only a handful of relatives and friends for audience. On our way back down to the rivers we again passed the old man, still there on the wall with his patient Brittany. As we walked past he touched his cap and smiled.

Then there was a long lunch on the terrace of a hotel restaurant in Le Bugue, the light through the sheltering trees waving over us and the families for whom this clearly was part of the Sunday ritual. The whole scene reminded me strongly of paintings by Renoir and Manet of the *guinguettes* (rural taverns) and garden parties where the sun was always shining on the hats and parasols of the diners, dancers, and drinkers. In this old country with its rich artistic tradition, life will imitate art around almost any bend in the road, as it was doing for me here once again.

So it was late afternoon when we got to Bara-Bahau, high in an oak forest above Le Bugue. The guide, a youngish woman, was obviously weary at this end-of-the-weekend hour, but we would be her last customers, and she summoned a brave smile and an even braver enthusiasm and showed us through the heavy door and down the steps to the cave floor that was slick with antediluvian water. "You must hold the railings at all times," she cautioned us as we began our tour with an almost casual glance at a low Gallo-Roman wall and lighted display cases in which were arrangements of marine fossils, bears' teeth and bones, and pot shards. Here, under a few feet of dusty glass, was a fabulous stretch of time, and passing it so cursorily, I wondered how we could do so: It was the sort of thing you felt you ought to kneel down before in profound awe and reverence, and yet you didn't.

This wall and case, as it turned out, was a fitting introduction to Bara-Bahau, because although it wasn't a huge cave like Rouffignac, there was a great deal to admire in its relatively restricted space, a feeling of density about it. Here was virtually the entire experience of the planet, from foraminifera right up to the dim light of a day we could recognize as our own in the remains of that Gallo-Roman wall. And there was something symbolically appropriate, too, in the fact that the cave had resisted definitive interpretation since it had been discov-

ered in 1951. Our guide told us scholars could not seem to figure out its chronology: the style of some of the engravings on
its friable walls looked archaic enough to suggest that here at
last you beheld the very dawn of Art. Yet Leroi-Gourhan
thought them much later than that, though they were oddly
"primitive" in style. He very tentatively assigned a date of
±14,000 years ago.

In the local dialect the site's name meant something like
"Falling Rocks That Make a Noise," perhaps a vague reference
to a pre-discovery legend where local people dropped rocks
through a fissure here, trying to sound the depths. In any case,
the name led our guide to tell us that our way into the sanctuary was not the entrance the ancient artists had used, which
long ago had been blocked by rockslides. That made me wonder yet again how many caves in this region had been sealed up
by similar occurrences and of these how many contained art
that might extend our appreciation of this tradition—or even
wholly revolutionize it. The conjectured original entrance
meant that those who came in here more than ten thousand
years ago would have had to crawl through a very narrow aper-
ture. And once inside, the artists would have had to kneel or
in some places even lie on their backs to execute their engravings of horses, aurochs, a huge, leaping bear, a rampant human
male genitalia. Then there was the great bison I'd read about
and wanted especially to see. It was fully worth the trip—massive, dense, alive with shaggy Ice Age life. The grand, burly
antiquity of this creature, surely related to those prehistoric
ones found in the New World whose bones and horns dwarf
those of our "modern" *Bison bison*, made me wince inwardly

when I fleetingly reflected on our casual, callous slaughter of the vast herds of the nineteenth century. That had been, I cynically supposed, an early and instructive example of the "wise use" approach to the environment.

There were also numerous geometric signs placed in what has been interpreted as strategic proximity to the animals. Some of these have been read as gender identifications, and others as indications of huts or group shelters. Still others might be territorial markings, akin to those esoteric and often elegant gang graffiti you see on the urban walls your train or car whips you past.

At other sites I'd seen another kind of territorial marking, the deep striations the cave bears made as they heaved themselves high above human height to claw the cave walls. Here they were everywhere, long, deeply grooved markings on surfaces that have often been described in the literature on Bara-Bahau as having the consistency of cheese. I didn't know what the bears had really been doing when they did this, whether they'd been marking territory, or simply stretching their claws after a winter's hibernation. But at this tremendous remove in which our perspective is both lengthened and distorted as well, it must seem to us almost as if the animals we depicted had sat for their portraits and afterwards marked their approval next to the finished product:

The Bear, His Mark

And maybe such a thought occurred to the ancient artists also. Maybe the daily proximity to the other creatures engendered that feeling of authentic kinship that was part of the more encompassing sense of undifferentiated grace. We are continually cautioned by scholars that it is always dangerous to extrapolate from the information on the cultures of historic peoples back to prehistoric ones; these imagined equivalencies, the scholars say, are likely to be just that. Still, in the surviving tatters of American Indian myths and legends you do find this sense of kinship with the animals and also a sense of responsibility, too: that humans were under sacred obligation to faithfully represent other animate forms of life in their stories, in their rites, in their dances and hunting customs. And it is the loss of this sense of kinship that forms the most poignant part of the worldwide myth of the Fall.

The notion that the bear or the bison might have sat for its portrait had, I thought, given me my imaginative entrance into Bara-Bahau. For it seemed to me, as we exited through the small lobby with its postcards and replica spear points, that even though our ways into the temple caves were made easy by lobbies and literature, guides, lights, and handrails, we still had our own kinds of difficulties in discovering authentic access, still had to find our own ways of confronting these mysterious places proving at last equal to the opportunity.

LA FERRASSIE

La Ferrassie might be the most significant site yet known in defining who the Neanderthals were and what they were in the process of becoming before they mysteriously vanished from Europe ±30,000 years ago. The site is not down on many maps, including some pretty detailed ones, and this must be because there is so little to look at there. First investigated in 1896, then again in 1902, and still further in the 1960s, its treasures have long since been transported to various museums and collections. These treasures were considerable and covered a period from the Middle Paleolithic period down to the period in which the great cave art was created. Here were found two fairly complete skeletons of adults and fragments of half a dozen infants and children. From my point of view, perhaps the most significant finds were bits of ochre, the favored coloring material of the Cro-Magnons; some plaques of limestone that appeared to have been intentionally placed in connection with the bodies;

and a curious limestone plaque with some small, cuplike indentations. No one knows quite what to make of these items, but they have generated heated debate—quite in keeping for a people about whom little is known and who have so long served us as a convenient image for all that is low-brow and dull-witted.

The site itself doesn't, as I say, seem to repay the effort you might make to find it: a roadside marker above Le Bugue and behind it a high wire fence enclosing part of the excavated complex. Beyond it rise limestone hills studded with oaks and chestnuts, and that seems to be all. But I wanted to look on the place of those burials, see the hills from which, presumably, those tantalizingly mysterious limestone plaques had come, especially that one with the finger-sized indentations. What could its possible use(s) have been for this people who had been long established here when the first Cro-Magnon pioneers came into the country and who shared it with them for thousands of years?

There wasn't any place to safely park the rented Mercedes right there at the site. So, I drove past it, up the slow rise of the rural road, until I found a branching dirt lane that rose and dipped through meadows and copses, and I parked there in the shade of trees that remained full-leafed in what was the most spectacularly beautiful stretch of French weather I'd ever experienced. Walking back down to the site across a meadow that smelled more of summer than autumn, I came to a small pond, jade green under willows, and on its other side, directly across from La Ferrassie, a stone washbasin almost swallowed in grass, where country washerwomen would once have bent battered knees over their work. Another part of the long story.

I didn't know precisely what I was expecting to find at the site itself—certainly not its long-gone treasures. Most often when I make such pilgrimages I don't. I know only I'm drawn like a dowser's wand to places where *something has happened*: some luminous portion of the story of life on our planet. Almost always I'm rewarded in ways I could never have anticipated. At Sand Creek, Colorado, for instance, where the Methodist elder Col. John Chivington cut down the Cheyenne peace chief Black Kettle, as he stood in front of his village holding an American flag, Elise and I found a medicine bundle, placed there by someone who wanted to remember that disgraceful day in 1864. In that dry, windswept moment on an unfeatured stretch of landscape past and present came thunderously together for us and we were given an understanding of what had brought us there.

It doesn't invariably happen, of course, which might mean nothing more than you weren't sufficiently alive to the opportunity. At this moment at La Ferrassie, though I felt I had my antennae out, not much was happening for me. There was the marker, the fence, the bland bit of landscape within it, tidied up after years of patient sifting and a low stone buttress shoring up the hillside that had been turned over for its treasures. Everything was right in front of me, evidently, and that "everything" seemed so negligible that it crossed my mind to simply turn away for another more promising place. There were so many hereabouts.

There was a path, though, just down the road from the marker, and it beckoned me to follow it into the trees and the green gloom that yet had a kind of luminescence to it, as if lit from within. As always in such situations, I had my eyes more on the earth just ahead of my steps rather than on the longer view. You missed things this way, of course, the larger picture, but there was always a tradeoff in the potential discovery of some detail you might never have noticed. Presently, I found myself stopping to look at three stones that lay in a suggestive triangle in the middle of the path. A bit of rough, sandy limestone stuck its little snout up at me like one of the aged rhinos I'd seen depicted in the caves. Next to it lay a folded piece of hematite that at first glance looked as if it had been worked by human hands. Below these two stones was a larger one, a chunk of flint, and this one really did look as if it had been flaked and then casually tossed aside. I picked it up with the others and turned it about in my hands, letting a shaft of sunlight catch those suggestively beveled edges, wondering whether I truly held here an artifact of ancient industry. The more I turned it about, the more difficult it seemed to account for those long, shallow grooves by some accidental means—avalanche, boulder-fall, torrential spill of the creek that fed the pond and the old washbasin in the meadow below. I put the stones in my pocket, where I kept rubbing them like rabbits' feet as I went on, the woods closing around me, the smell of the shade-dampened earth rising into my nostrils. I hadn't gone far when I caught a dark something out of the corner of my eye, and instantly, my dream of a Neanderthal discovery flashed to mind. It was the entrance to a cave.

All about it were strewn rocks that looked very much as though they'd been tossed there by whoever had once excavated it, but so long ago that they'd grown beards of moss. A fragile webbing of vines trailed across the dark entrance which I could now see sloped steeply down and then took a sharp left-handed twist. I knew that archeologists, speleologists, and paleontologists routinely prospected for other possible entrances around cave sites of any significance, and I stood there wondering whether what I was looking at was the residue of such an effort. The La Ferrassie complex was certainly large enough and important enough to have had experts digging about this far up from the road and the rock shelter that had first drawn their attention. Possessed by that dream, I saw myself feeling my way along a tunnel, down-slope, following a maze-way hallowed by the tracks of a mysteriously vanished people. But just as quickly I saw the impracticality of the idea (I had no flashlight) as well as its hazard, and I remembered the legend of Floyd Collins, fatally trapped in a Kentucky cave in 1925. I was by myself here, far from home, and no one knew my daily plans. So, I simply stood above the vine-webbed entrance, not quite idly tossing a few rocks down the hole to hear what I could.

In this spot I was bound to think once again of the beautifully suggestive fact that those who had discovered Chauvet Cave in the Ardèche had done so by moving slowly and with infinite care along the limestone slopes, pressing their faces to holes and fissures in hopes of catching the breath of the earth that would tell them they might be poised atop some great possibility. Finally, their quest had been rewarded, spectacularly so; they had lived out their great dream. And what was that dream, finally, but the radically human one of having some authentic contact with our essential and irrefragable nature? To drop down into that well of the Past that Thomas Mann had said was fathomless but which *must* have a flooring somewhere: down there below the desiccated evidences of the first farmers; below the temple caves; beneath the first campsites, the stains of the oldest hearths, the narrow tread left by our most remote ancestors in Africa, striding across an open space that had been bright with promise and peril. . . .

The Neanderthals for whom this had been the heartland and who left their bones and tools in these hills had themselves been products of that deep and unfathomed past that extended back beyond even their beginnings, though it was difficult to keep this in mind since their image has been so primitive it seemed they must stand at the very dawn of Time itself. Yet they were inheritors of morphological developments immeasurably more ancient than they. And now we have learned that even if they may have been the human pioneers of this region, they were certainly not the first-comers into what we now call Europe.

At the beginning of the twentieth century–less than a nanosecond in the scale of these matters–*Homo heidelbergensis* was believed to be the pioneering hominid species in Europe, coming into the continent ±500,000 years ago. Now even greater depths have been sounded with the excavations at Sierra de Atapuerco in northernmost Spain. In the mid-1990s finds there of human remains and hundreds of stone tools there have pushed the frontiers of Old World hominid occupation back beyond *Homo heidelbergensis* to human beings who lived more than 850,000 years ago—this compared to the conjectured European advent of the Neanderthals at ±200,000 years ago. *Homo antecessor*, as the Atapuerca people are currently called, is now regarded by some researchers as the common ancestor of *Heidelbergensis*, the Neanderthals, and the fully modern humans. These were big-brained hunters and gatherers like the Neanderthals and the Cro-Magnons. And like them too they manifested evidence of symbolic thought in crude but unmistakable burials of their dead. In addition to hunting the outsized animals of their epoch, they likely gathered plants to supplement their diet of flesh, which included the flesh and brain matter of their own kind.

They were primarily though not exclusively cave dwellers it seems, possibly a dim mnemonic echo of that moment in evolutionary time when *their* ancestors had lived in the shelter provided by forest canopies. And maybe in coming into this country the Neanderthals, too, had been remembering in obscure but telling ways the old sheltered life in Africa and so had naturally taken to caves and rocky overhangs. Standing there at the mouth of the sort of shelter that had served so many of the ancestors, I had to wonder whether the whole line of hominids and not merely *Homo sapiens sapiens* wasn't genetically fitted out with that retrospective impulse Rilke had written about so beautifully; whether here in these hills the Neanderthals too had looked back over their shoulders towards some imagined paradise where life had been easier and they had felt a kinship with everything that was. And here I was, a descendant of the race that succeeded the Neanderthals, and I was looking back, too. Why else was I here? Everything in my makeup, my structure, my braincase, my in-built predilection for retrospective thought—all of this had come to me out of the lives lived by the vanished peoples of this place. At that moment I felt I was so close to the foundations of the Past that I could reach out and touch them, that I had in fact pieces of them in my pocket—those stones. It suddenly seemed clear to me that I hadn't *chosen* this quest. It had been chosen for me, ordained, by virtue of who I was, how I'd been made. I'd been *sent* here, to Aquitaine, and to this very spot within it.

That summons had been issued years ago, but I had resisted it then. On the night of May 18–19, 1999, I'd been awakened in a Paris hotel room by a dream in which a voice had very distinctly said, "For I am called to speak of the beautiful and archaic earth." I had been sufficiently impressed by this to note it the next morning in my journal, but then I had gone on to other, more immediate literary tasks. Yet it had stayed with me. Now, suddenly, as I stood at the mouth of the cave, here it was again, both summons and prophecy, too, telling me that I must still find a way of speaking of the ancestors and of that beautiful and archaic earth we shared. We are moving pieces animated by the memory of everything that has gone into our making, the writer John N. Bleibtreu once observed. "For each of us as we pass from nonbeing into being, there moves with us like the tail of a comet . . . remembrances of time-past." Thus the dead "move among us the living, with their accomplishments alive in our flesh." I couldn't know in any precise way how the accomplishments of those who might possibly have used this cave had been communicated to me. I was only certain at this moment that somehow they had been.

No one has yet explained just why the Neanderthals died out, disappeared from the landscape of Ice Age Europe, or what if anything their accomplishments might mean for us the living who walk in their footsteps. They could not have simply withered away, you think, for these were tremendously resourceful and adaptive human beings, very far indeed from the dull-witted brutes of caricature. They survived through ages of drastic climatic swings that were the consequence of the advances and retreats of the ice caps. We have evidence of at least seventeen of these: changes in air and water temperature; in the configuration of shorelines; in the relationship and extent of forest and tundra; and the extinction and disappearance of various animal species. Plainly, dealing with all this took brains, and they had big ones, as big or bigger than ours. Nor were they the brutish-looking creatures pictured throughout much of the last century, with huge brow ridges, flat skulls, receding chins. More recent reconstructions of their faces and forms make them appear more nearly like the newcomers who eventually came to dominate—and to decorate, too—the old Neanderthal homeland. Why then did they disappear?

Some claim the newcomers killed them off, not in pitched battles, but gradually, incrementally, relentlessly, until finally their numbers had dwindled to that point where they were no longer a biologically viable people, reminiscent of the process whereby Europeans so speedily whittled down and isolated remnants of the American Indian tribes of New England and California. The Cro-Magnons were able to do this, some say, because they were far more accomplished artisans, crafting weapons and tools that were more lethal and efficient than those of the natives. With what we know—and with what the news daily reinforces with a numbing constancy—about our capacities for violence and the destruction of whole groups, we can't dismiss this theory out of hand.

Other scholars, noting that same superiority of Cro-Magnon weapons and tools, say it was less a matter of killing off the natives than it was of the Cro-Magnons' simply out-competing the Neanderthals for the available resources. And still others say the critical skill that ultimately tipped the balance in favor of the newcomers was the Cro-Magnons' far greater communication skills. Whether the Neanderthals had a language as we would understand the term has long been a subject of debate. But comparative studies of facial and throat structures suggest that speech may have been considerably easier for the Cro-Magnons than the natives. Greater language skills would obviously confer immeasurable advantages on the group that had them. On the eve of Spain's conquest of the New World the court lexicographer to Queen Isabella pithily put the case for compiling a new dictionary by telling her, "Language, Your Highness, is the perfect instrument of empire."

But then there is the matter of Art, and here the issue of relative communication skills seems a good deal more clear-cut. The art of the Cro-Magnons was highly sophisticated, technically masterful, esthetically brilliant. It also clearly fulfilled important non-esthetic cultural functions. In other words, as Randall White has said, the art had major "practical" values for the people who practiced it and witnessed it, too. We don't know what its specific functions were, but we do know that in ways now lost to Time the cave paintings and engravings and portable statuettes helped the Cro-Magnons survive and prosper in their world, that it was not purely and solely decorative, though this in itself would also be a function. So far as is now known, though, the Neanderthals never drew or painted on cave walls. It is possible, therefore, that their relative lack of artistic skills had something to do with their eventual disappearance, that their human competitors received and communicated vital information through Art that the natives couldn't. Artists are the antennae of the race, Ezra Pound said, and in this instance the metaphor is powerfully suggestive.

Whatever the truth of this may be, there is an emerging body of scientific thought that can easily enough accommodate the various speculations about relative cultural skills. This holds that the Cro-Magnons gradually incorporated the Neanderthals, culturally and biologically.

For years it has been vehemently denied by many leading paleoanthropologists that there was interbreeding between Cro-Magnons and Neanderthals. Now, though, that determined theoretical resistance shows signs of breaking down, and some geneticists and population biologists are saying there was and that the genetic signature of the latter lives on as a shadowy trace in present-day humans. True, interbreeding and consequent incorporation would not by itself sufficiently account for the disappearance of the Neanderthals. But in some combination with the greater technical and communication skills of the newcomers it might tell us a good deal more of the story.

Under the direction of the eminent paleoanthropologist, Ian Tattersall of the American Museum of Natural History, scientists have painstakingly pieced together a skeletal model of a Neanderthal male. Placed alongside a *Homo sapiens* skeleton, it is clear there were distinct structural differences. And yet, as another specialist, Erik Trinkaus of Washington University, points out, these differences would have been invisible to the people themselves in their encounters in the landscape of Ice Age Europe. They would not, he thinks, have noticed the different body conformations, the Neanderthals' broader trunks, the Cro-Magnons' longer forearms. They certainly couldn't have noticed the Neanderthals' larger hyoid bone anchoring the muscles of the tongue to other parts of the vocal mechanism. They would instead have recognized one another as human beings with the easily imagined consequences that now, millennia onward, survive in our molecular makeup.

Over the summer months when I'd been doing the background reading for my quest, the more I thought about it, the more unlikely it seemed that there had been no interbreeding during the thousands of years these groups had shared this very landscape. The question of interaction is cast into even higher relief when the inquiry is extended to include the period before the Cro-Magnons migrated into Europe, because in the Levant they shared that region with the Neanderthals for an even longer period.

It would be silly, of course, to imagine the natives had welcomed the newcomers to their heartland and showed them around. I thought the novelist William Golding's fictional reconstruction of their primitive encounters far more likely. In *The Inheritors*, Golding imagined the mingled fear and fascination the Neanderthals might have felt in their first, accidental encounters with those who looked so much like themselves and yet behaved in distinctly different ways. But it would be equally silly to imagine that over millennia the two peoples hadn't come to see that they had many things in common. Right from the moment of first contact they would have been struck by the fact of their common bipedalism and that digital dexterity that distinguished them both from all the other creatures. And the longer they lived in the same landscape, the more things they would have come to have in common, though it seems likely that the natives might have taken more from the newcomers than the other way around.

Both had cosmologies of some sort. The evidence of Cro-Magnons' is so abundant it needs no argument. Less well-known and harder to delineate is that of the Neanderthals'. Yet the evidence is there, and it was what had brought me to this particular site and was pulling me farther into their woods. Erik Trinkaus has convincingly demonstrated that Neanderthals cared for the wounded (and therefore probably for the infirm as well). La Ferrassie indicated ritual burials.

These practices would seem to presuppose some theory or vision of human life and destiny that transcends the merely mortal and observable. Most likely the practices had the same genesis as the Cro-Magnons' cognate ones and their decoration of the caves: the apprehension of Death and the simultaneous affirmation of the Life Force.

How many millennia it took before the Neanderthals came to the understanding that Death was not just the destiny of the creatures they killed but was theirs as well is an impossible line of speculation. We know only that they eventually came to it. We know this because of their compassion for the infirm and their concern for the journey to some other sphere beyond our own. We know also that for them, as for the Cro-Magnons, Art came to serve as some kind of mediator between them and Death. The Neanderthals may not have painted or drawn the animals, but they used ochre and manganese oxide, probably for body decoration, and they used them before the coming of the Cro-Magnons. They pierced animal teeth, and 36,000 years ago they wore ornaments. Art, even in rudimentary forms such as a child's scribble, arrests Time, if only for an instant, abrogates it, takes hold of destiny and reshapes it into contours and colors gratifying to the human heart. Every creature, Freud famously claimed, wants to die on its own terms, and in arresting Time and abrogating it, Art helps humans do that. It is our champion, in there in the valiant, beautifully doomed contest with Old Death. Art was this for the Neanderthals as it was for their successors, whose far greater facility with manganese, moss, ochre, and bone left us these almost imperishable works.

Trying to visualize both the cultural and physical consequences of the coming together of the Neanderthals and the Cro-Magnons here in these hills, I turned away from the cave and whatever might lie within its shaggy recesses and rejoined the upward path, feeling myself now in the company of Neanderthal spirits, not those of the newcomers whose art had been preoccupying my days and filtering into my dreams and sleepless moments at night. Shortly, the path narrowed and then opened out into a small upland meadow filled with waving clover and Queen Anne's lace. On its far side, through the trees, I caught a glimpse of a dark, semi-oval that I thought might be another cave, but I kept to the path, past the meadow to where blackberry bushes bent over the way, the boughs heavy with luscious fruit. I gathered a handful and continued on, crunching the berries with molars about half the size of those the Neanderthals had had.

Once more the path narrowed, and the woods closed around me. Bird calls echoed off trunks and branches, and the leaves underfoot lay in thick drifts. Far off there sounded the muffled crack of a hunter's gun, reminding me both of the ancient hunters who may never have developed the notion of sport and also of the fact that I myself was here a hunter of sorts. A few minutes later, still climbing and the oaks beginning to give way to chestnuts and pines, I spotted something white through the trees and then found it was a small van. It had to have come down from somewhere above because no vehicle could have come up my path. Then I saw the man who'd driven it, and supposing him to be the hunter whose gun I'd heard down below, I called out a hearty *"Bonjour!"* as a precaution. He stopped stock-still behind a tree. Then, seeing me, he stepped cautiously forward, looking narrowly at the notebook and pen I carried in one hand. I saw then that he wasn't a hunter but a woodcutter with a stack of cut pine logs piled next to the van and his two-stroke saw visible through the opened cargo doors. He was a squirrel-faced, narrow-eyed fellow wearing a much-faded t-shirt that proclaimed him an "Amazon Jungle Explorer." But who was I, this white-haired *mec* (guy) with writing materials?

I smiled steadily as I came on, and when we were face-to-face he asked, *"Anglais?"* still looking hard at that notebook so that I suddenly wondered whether he was up here not just cutting wood but poaching it.

"Non, je suis Americain." This seemed to perplex him even more. What would an American be doing up in these woods at this time of year? Maybe down below in Le Bugue in high summer, but not now or here. Brits, on the other hand, might turn up just about anywhere, at any season. I felt therefore that I had to add something further in the way of explanation and so blundered on. *"Je suis écrivain, ah, ecrivant sur les gens préhistoriques. Vous savez, les Cro-Magnons: les artistes et chasseurs anciens."* Still no light of comprehension in his face. Maybe my caveman French was confusing him, and so when he made no further response but only continued his hard staring I stepped carefully around him, wondering fleetingly if I ought to stop a few steps away and make some scribble in my notebook as visible evidence of my harmless intentions. But

I just kept walking, feeling his eyes boring into my back and oddly wishing I hadn't used that word, *"préhistorique,"* which in any language I was coming to distrust and which in this particular instance had probably only confused the issue. In another minute or so, I turned about and found him lost from view.

But the word stayed with me. What did it really mean, anyway? In common usage, of course, it was used to designate all of human history for which no written records exist, which in point of fact makes up most of the story. History picks up–it doesn't actually *begin*–with the records marked on the clay tablets of the ancient Near East narrating the rise of the literate city-states. But most of the human story had been lived before then, and *all* of the evolutionary work that went into the making of the human animal had been accomplished. On this path I was literally in the footsteps of those who'd learned to control fire, to hunt and gather, to shape spear points and to shape vocal sounds into articulate speech; who had come to bury their dead with ritual viaticum; to draw and paint and sculpt; and to honor the other creatures as their fellows.

Maybe the Near Eastern city-states did constitute the first "high civilizations," as the term is understood. But the humans of "prehistory" certainly had their own kinds of civilization, rudimentary as these must have been, and today there are deep ecologists following the lead of the late Paul Shepard who believe our Cro-Magnon ancestors were more fully, radically human than their city-centered successors. If the mission of humans on earth is to remember everything of the long story, to remember to remember, as Henry Miller has it, then that mission must begin with our rememberings of those who moved through this landscape in the eons before there were letters. History did not begin at Sumer—to use the title of a once-famous book. Indeed, evidently the Sumerians themselves didn't believe this. Philologists tell us that their term for the future meant something like "that which is found behind one's back," while their term for the past indicated that which you could see in front of you. This suggests they saw themselves as part of a historical continuum rather than the originators of it. History was the repetition of the past. History didn't begin at La Ferrassie either, or even at Blombos Cave in South Africa. But La Ferrassie was certainly much closer to the sources of our being than Sumer, and we needed, I thought, very much to take it as fully into account as we could.

It wasn't so much a matter of a purely historical accuracy. Rather it was a matter of a more inclusive *emotional* understanding of who we are, of all that has gone into the making of us: of the long, dimly understood foreground that prepared the way for those who eventually came to see animals as commodities, not as emissaries of the powers, and to lift water from its natural courses into the fields of grain. Whether these spectacular cultural innovations rendered the Sumerians and their successors somehow less human than the Cro-Magnons is a highly debatable point. But maybe Paul Shepard's point, more generally taken, was that our hunter ancestors were a great deal nearer the sources of nature than those who followed them. And maybe the further point was that when we begin our understanding of the human story with the recorders of history we forget certain essential things about ourselves as a species, about the planet we inhabit.

I was nearing something different myself now, mundane though it was, walking the tire ruts left by the woodcutter's van. The woods were opening out from the green air of the chestnuts into the ordered rows of a pine plantation, like a metaphor of the great transition from hunting to agriculture. Here the path became a dirt road, and I walked south along it, out of the pine rows and into the sun and the apple trees of a little farm. Below the farmhouse lay a meadow in the middle of which sat an old stone hut with a slate roof that fitted it like a peasant's hat. A gnarled apple tree, long unpruned, struggled up above the pitch of the roof, and there were a few apples on its boughs and a ladder leaning against the trunk. Here, I thought, was the microcosmic image of that transition, that part of the story that followed from the last days of the hunters and the mighty herds that once coursed through this now-domesticated landscape. For when the retreat of the ice caps was at last complete and the herds had followed them northward, then the hunters had had to learn new skills in a warmer, less-wild world. They turned—very quickly, too—to the tilling of the earth, to planting, to planning, to harvesting, storing, and herding.

They accomplished this stupendous transformation in about 5,000 years, this after millions of years as hunters and gatherers. And nowhere was the revolution more tellingly registered than in Art. The art of the high civilizations of the ancient Near East speaks to us of that inexhaustible fount of human creativity—new forms, new techniques, new subjects. It speaks to us also of our changed attitudes about ourselves and about the earth. Whereas the human figure is so definitely subordinate to the animals in Paleolithic art, in Neolithic art we find the human figure omnipresent—queens and goddesses, square-bearded kings and gods—the postures of the figures radiating a confidence and even an arrogance previously unseen. Even more startling is the evolution of the animals in Near Eastern art. They have become domesticated. They are our servants, not divine emissaries. The horse now wears a collar and bridle, the bull has a human beard or wears a handle on his back so that he can serve as a desk weight, a new household item of literate cultures.

To Paul Shepard's disciples this was the actual, historical Fall, from a paradise of hunting into a grubby mercenary world where the ceaseless toil of agriculture fulfilled the biblical curse that humans were doomed to earn their bread by the sweat of their brow. In this view, it was an inevitable step from tilling and herding to the fencing off of private property and the herding of human chattel. Maybe.

But maybe our desacrilized, urbanized world of the West seduces us here into a warped view of the world of the ancient hunters. We are seduced most significantly by the art of the caves, but also by the severe elegance of Magdalenian harpoons where love and death are wedded in the cruel beauty of the points and barbs; and by the voluptuousness of the Venus figurines where somehow everything seems comprehended, all contradictions subsumed. Because, of course, there was more to that world than the beauty of its art and artifacts. There was great terror as well as great beauty there, and the art and artifacts tell us this. The hunters who made the images and shaped the spears might have lived in a kind of prelapsarian paradise where they felt in intimate contact with everything and with the Powers that ruled the cosmos. But that sort of daily intimacy must also have contained within it the fear of being utterly consumed, annihilated, by such intimate contact with the Powers. When we make the effort to take the art as seriously as its makers must have, we feel at least something of this—or ought to. When we forget what went into the beauty we admire in the art and artifacts, we forget something essential of ourselves.

As for myself, I had to admit there was now an odd psychic relief in looking down on the ordered and familiar shapes of meadowland and farm and apple trees, as if I had emerged not from merely a stretch of woods but instead from out of that ancient hunters' world with its dark powers and gigantic beasts, its caves and mighty rivers and wintry tundra. "Very deep is the well of the past," wrote Thomas Mann. "Should we not call it bottomless?" In climbing through the green and leaf-moldy woods I had actually felt myself descending into that bottomless well of the past, as I had first at Rouffignac and virtually every day since. Here at the upland farm I felt I had come up for air and stood once more in the simple sun with the great weight of ages shifted for a moment from my shoulders. And I was pleased to remember in these moments, not the Ice Age art and its world but the words of an artist of my own time and place.

In the 1970s, the Italian artist Gianfranco Baruchello had made a philosophically based retreat from the city to a farm probably not unlike this one I now gazed on. There, like my old hero Thoreau, he had learned to till the earth and to focus his fullest attentions on the soil of this planet that we'd been given to love and to live on. Baruchello hardly shared the view of those deep ecologists who believed the life of the hunter represented humanity's truest state and farming the fall into money-grubbing and an adversarial relationship with nature. Quite the opposite. Having retreated from the city, Baruchello found the farm a place where he could realign his values and rededicate himself to Art in the widest and deepest sense. A human, he finally found, is "supposed to learn to apply at least an intelligent selection of the Ten Commandments, about seven of them I guess would do, and then he's supposed to sing and to love, and then to make poetry, cultivate the earth and raise his children to do the same."

That sounded about right to me.

THE WEIGHT OF THE PAST

＞—І—◆＞—〇—＜◆—І—＜

When I came out of L'Abri Cap Blanc into the surreal-seeming light of the present it was past mid-day. By now I had come to understand that after an immersion in the Paleolithic past you had to allow some time to get your land legs under you once again, to move about in the world of automobiles, parking lots, and people dressed more or less like yourself. So I stood there in the leafy, rocky shade for a few minutes, staring fairly stupidly at the bicycles of the group with whom I'd gone into the rock shelter: These contraptions looked so bizarre to me after the experience within that I found myself almost wondering what they might be for. But shortly things came together again, and I moved off toward my car as the riders mounted those bikes and pumped up the steep slope to the road.

My intention was to drive from here north along the valley of the Vézère to Le Thot, where there was a zoological park with a few Przewalski's horses in it. Some believe these creatures may be related to the horses depicted in the famous sculptures I'd just encountered at Cap Blanc, a work more than forty feet long and dated ±12,500 years old. On my travels I've found it true that "nothing good happens on a main road," as an old Kansas goat-herder once told me, and I knew there were back roads up to Le Thot. But I'd already gotten good and turned about in this country of ancient winding lanes, along which directions could be both scarce and ambiguous. Just last evening, coming up in the dusk from Sarlat, I'd gotten so hopelessly confused trying to find Jean and Nicole Querre's place in St.-Crépin that I'd asked the same young man three times for directions. The first two times he'd been obliging. The third time he'd just kept on raking his leaves without glancing up.

So now, I decided to go back the safe way, the way I knew, coming down to Font-de-Gaume Cave where I'd spent the morning and then picking up the D 706 at Les Eyzies, which would give me a straight shot up the Vézère to the park.

The road back down crossed a small, sun-bright meadow with a line of poplars along one edge. Dead ahead you had a fine, comprehensive view of the Font-de-Gaume site, a great stone spearhead projecting toward the river valley with a luxuriant chestnut forest atop it. I'd noted this same meadow on my mission to Cap Blanc and had thought–fleetingly, almost guiltily–"Hell of a spot for a picnic." Now here was its temptation once again. "No sane man can afford to dispense with debilitating pleasures," the grand gourmet A. J. Liebling once wrote, and as I had long sought sanity by the road of excess, Liebling came handily to me now, and I felt the meadow was practically buttonholing me, telling me to stop awhile. But not without provisions, surely.

So, when I returned to it from Les Eyzies I had a small round of *cabecou* (the local goat cheese), a *ficelle* (small, narrow baguette), and a sturdy '99 Margaux. There had been a heavy fog in the valley that morning, and I found the grasses still damp from it here and there, but eventually I came to a slight, west-facing slope the sun had dried, not far from the straight shadows the poplars were beginning to throw eastward across the small, enclosed expanse. There I sat down and "poured out the wine for the high invisible ones," as Yeats had written, and I thought, almost involuntarily by this point, of the invisible ones surrounding me in this valley. I raised my converted jelly glass to Font-de-Gaume, looming high in the autumn air with its dark, glistening mane of chestnuts, and drank a toast in gratitude to it and to those who had decorated it. Then I spread out the rest of my provisions, hearing the late-season dry whisper of the grasses and finding, up close, how many of them were at last taking on the sere tan of winter dormancy. In fact, much of the landscape was beginning to show the season despite this prolonged mellowness. This morning, coming down from St.-Crépin, I'd swung past a tiny vineyard where the leaves hung black and lifeless-looking, their moment spent. And then in the fog-shrouded valley, I'd waited in a sharp chill with a few other ticketless supplicants for the office to open at Font-de-Gaume, feeling the lateness of the fall and sensing the keen, inexorable advance of the next season while morning traffic whipped shawls of fog into our faces. When the wicket opened at last I was almost as grateful for the warmth I felt coming from it as for the ticket I was able to get.

Inside Font-de-Gaume, though, it had been no colder than at the waiting area below and certainly not as cold as at the bottom of the chasmal Rouffignac. When the Abbé Breuil made a scrupulous inventory of the cave in the last century he found its layout and decorations so classic he designated it one of the Six Giants (along with Lascaux, Altamira, Niaux, Les Combarelles, and Les Trois-Frères). You entered it to find little that was remarkable until you reached a point where the walls narrowed (subsequently dubbed the "Rubicon") and beyond which there was a sprinkling of the mysterious red dots. Clearly this was a point of initiation to what lay within, the art of the inner chambers. In these you encountered the procession of the animals—steppe bison, rhinos, horses, reindeer, woolly mammoths, and a few felines. There were numerous tectiform signs spaced about, too, but these didn't draw me nearly as much as the animals did. Finally, you passed beneath the steady, ageless stare of the creatures, toward the far recesses of the cave, and there you found one of the "ghosts," like those found at three of the other "giants." It looked like this:

—F. T.

Beyond the ghost, on the last wall were seven long red strokes, splaying out in vaguely fanlike fashion.

The whole thing seemed to Breuil almost *clearly* laid out, whatever its constituent mysteries. You entered from the light of the quotidian world, persevering in darkness and faith to where the walls seemed to threaten you; there you passed over into the real world where the spirit forms of the animals were evoked in paintings and engravings out of the living rock. At this depth you were compelled to see, and also to surrender, to the spirit essence that lay hidden within the animals that in the world outside were prey: meat, clothing, solvents, materials for tools and shelter. In here they sloughed off their utilitarian guises to become their truer selves. Looking once again at that daring felicity of line, the racy economy of it, it came to me more clearly than ever that this was far more than mere style or mastery, another instance of the great tradition. It was those things, of course. But it seemed to me more significantly to have been a strategy of guidance, of tutelage for the audience, taking them past the animals' utilitarian guises and into their numinous presence. And in the audience's surrender to this deeper layer—one the artists' technical facility had made possible—lay salvation. Because in the numinous lay the truth, *the way things really were*—and are. The cave's layout and the decorations that were fitted into it said to the people who came down here, "We are not the Lords of Creation, free to dispose of all things as best suits us. We are only a part of the Great Dance, and a small part at that."

This message, so beautifully rendered, was reinforced at the back of the cave, where the artists were literally running out of room. There the audience found depictions of themselves in a little alcove where two goblinesque outlines faced each other with big eyes, and there, too, was that blobby ghost that was all eyes. The comparison of these images with those of the creatures earlier encountered was meant to be humbling. So, it seems to me, was the exclusive emphasis on the eyes of these characters. How, we might well wonder, could we have been anything *other* than all eyes in the midst of such transcendent beauty as this world was and still is? For me, sitting in this meadow, in this sun, I could not help but think yet again of Thoreau, who kept trying to communicate to those he called the Johns and Jonathans of his time his awe of the natural world. Our habit of always looking heavenward for salvation blinds us to the truth, he said: heaven is right here, under our feet.

Nowhere was it more literally as well as metaphorically true than here in this country. Inside Font-de-Gaume and the other sacred sites, Ice Age peoples had been compelled to see this and to remember it outside the caves as well as they went about the often arduous tasks of staying well and keeping warm. And as I went about on my own task, my quest, I was compelled to do likewise. From the moment I struggled to full wakefulness in some unfamiliar room, I was forced into an ongoing engagement with what felt very much like the whole hoary narrative of earthly existence: with the art of the caves and shelters and their animals; with the "sorcerers," the vulvas and Venuses and playfully carved penises; with the rocky, flinty skin of the earth itself; with the central, governing fact that life feeds on death, visible both in the art and in the spear points and harpoons in the museums; with the almost immemorial story of warfare and the atrocities of which we are all capable; with the sublimities of religious aspiration which, like the churches and cathedrals rising above roofs and barns and businesses, aspired towards divinity.

Not only was I compelled to see all this and remember it by day, but by night as well, when my dreams were filled with jumbled images of caves and rocky overhangs, rivers, forests, and a million scattered flakes of flint falling through sleep like the superimposed outlines of the animals on the sanctuaries' walls and ceilings. So, during these weeks there were moments when it felt to me as if I had awakened only in the late shadows of my life from a long sleep; that I had never lived so intensely as a member of my species, never been so daily aware of what that meant. There were moments, too, when I found myself staring into the bathroom mirror of some hotel room and musing on the mysteries of morphology as reflected back at me: Why *didn't* I have horns like the sorcerer figures of Gabillou and Les Trois-Frères? The question had clearly occurred to my ancestors. And there were other sorts of moments as well, all born of this fabulous encounter, where it felt as if I might be overwhelmed and even crushed by the intensity of it all, by the opportunity I had to be so close to the sources of Art, civilization, our radical and common humanity.

This moment in the meadow was an intoxicating combination of all these feelings. I was still in the powerful grip of all I'd seen this day, at Font-de-Gaume and Cap Blanc. I was filled with the sun, the shadowy blue spires of the poplars, the wine, the goat cheese, the fresh and floury flavor of the *ficelle*. But there was something more here as well, the feeling that maybe I couldn't take too much more of this, that maybe I shouldn't. In the coming days I had in mind a return visit to Lascaux II and the adjacent site at Régourdou. Then my older son was to join me for a trip south to Niaux and its grand circular Black Salon. From there we planned to travel northeast to look at the country of the Ardèche, even though Jean Clottes had told me Chauvet Cave itself was so restricted even his wife had never been allowed inside it.

But now I began to wonder about the wisdom of such plans. Was I nearing that point at which I would be overburdened and my preciously accumulated impressions would begin to dissolve into a messy blur? When I was a boy in south Chicago my old swimming coach used to quote to me what he claimed was a motto of the Medes and Persians: "Too much is not enough. Not enough is plenty." I didn't think I had nearly enough of the country of the temple caves, but I knew also that another lifetime wouldn't give me enough either. Did I already have that quasi-cryptic "plenty" of the motto?

Whatever the case, there was no question that I had to clean up here and drive northward to the horses at Le Thot. Mostly, I had to see how they matched with those I'd seen at Cap Blanc under the ponderous yellow-white overhang: horses so fully rounded they appeared to be emerging out of the rock in a slow, metamorphic action of the ages that might, if only you had the time, finally be completed while you gazed. This strange impression was given further dimension by the fact that several of the horses appeared to have originally been carved as bison before the artists had decided they should finally be horses. Even the damage of the ages, including that of their discovery, added to the impression of shape-shifting, as where a portion of a figure had fallen away, leaving intact only part of the belly, rump, or legs. Here it looked less like damage than that the full figure had not yet emerged from the wall. If Ovid, that old mythographer, had known of Cap Blanc, surely he would have included it in his book on the marvels of worlds before his own.

If I were to write here that my drive up the Vézère was beautiful in the afternoon light, that would be true to life, but not faithful to the experience. The road rose and dipped, keeping company with the river. There were farmlands alternating with stands of oak as I went past Abri La Madeleine and Le Moustier, sites that had lent their names to whole epochs of the Paleolithic past; and then past Roque St.-Christophe, where Alain Querre and I had spent our first day in the country, a spot that might easily enough repay a full week's inspection. All this, as I say, would be truth about the road and where it took me. But I didn't really see it. I was instead focused on my next destination, which ought to have told me something.

Then I was at the park at Le Thot but saw as I pulled into its lot that something about the scene was amiss. There were only two vans there and their occupants were standing about with that mingled air of bafflement, irritation, and experienced resignation that in France signals some sort of *fermeture* (closing). This could be because of a *grève* (strike), a *fête* (holiday), or a *fermeture extraordinaire* (actual reason for closing never to be discovered). The veterans glanced at the newly arrived victim, rolled their eyes, and gave the Gallic shoulder shrug that here meant, "It's out of human control." And it really did seem to be so, the offices and attached museum dark and bolted and no sign anywhere of so much as a handyman to whom you might at least put a question.

The travelers in the vans were together, and now they left in tandem, towing their disappointment. But I had come a good deal farther than they, and I also smelled animals and hay and apples. I followed these scents down the lane behind park headquarters and found the source of them in an apple orchard and a series of pens within which were some of the animals associated in a general, thematic way with Ice Age peoples. All the gates were barred, of course, and there was a large, firmly worded sign warning you the park took no responsibility for trespassers. These were wild animals here, you were told, not pets.

Chicago boys of a half-century ago were experienced gatecrashers before they were out of junior high, at least the ones I hung out with: adept at vaulting turnstiles or slipping into ballparks while a friend engaged the usher with an innocent question about seating arrangements. So, here at the pens, old habit took over, and I was soon inside the high-barred gate and moving past an enclosure where some American bison glanced at me with clouded eyes. Beyond were the horses, three of them, standing in the shade of an open, tin-roofed shed, their tails toward me and their conformations impossible to assess from my angle.

Przewalski's horse, discovered in western Mongolia in the 1870s by a Russian explorer, was for some years believed to be the last subspecies of wild horse surviving into the twentieth century. Then in 1995 a French expedition into remote Tibet discovered a small, low-slung pony with black leg bars and dorsal stripe. Also wild, though living in comfortable proximity to the Bon-po people, the so-called Riwoche horse looked in photographs strikingly like some of those represented by the cave artists. So did Przewalski's horse as I'd seen it in photos, but these three weren't showing me anything but their butts. I shouted, whistled, waved my arms. The creatures stood stolid and still until I had the happy thought of lobbing some handy stones onto that roof they were using for shade.

When the first stone hit the roof and rattled down its grooves the horses spooked and trotted out into the sun, and as they came to a halt and looked back to the shed I saw one of them in splendid and revealing profile: the short arc of the neck, bristling mane, absence of forelock, the generous up-curve of the belly. The head was slightly Roman-nosed, the jaw full. These were precisely the features represented in the cave art, down to the black legs and tail. The only thing missing, so it seemed to me, was the beard sometimes indicated by the artists with bold hatchings, but even here, I thought, "I'd love to see these guys wearing their winter coats."

There's a numb literalism that lurks about the edges of any pilgrimage: seeing is believing. I have often been conscious of it on the many pilgrimages I've made, some to places where I well knew there could remain no least vestige of whatever it was that had happened there. Here at the pens, though I knew the identification of these horses with those of the caves was speculative, and though I felt that in some ways the Riwoche horse looked like a better match, these chunky fellows I'd spooked into the sun looked archaic enough to suit my need, which was to feel in what ways I could what had gone into this art of the ages. They had given me what I came for, too, and I stood there, hands on the fence rails, greedily drinking in their lines, noting what the artists had chosen to accentuate, like the curve of the belly, the answering arc of the neck. I thought I owed the horses something for having showed themselves to me in such fine detail and because I had disturbed with my stones a peaceful moment they'd been sharing under the shed. There were apples on the boughs of the trees just downhill from the pens, and I thought of fetching some, but then I felt they'd been thrown at enough for one afternoon, and so I left them to amble in good time back into the shade, as I was sure they soon would.

On my way up to Le Thot I'd noted a sign for Le Conquil, an ancient site that contained among other things a *pigeonnier* believed by some to have had an earlier life as a temple to Mithra, whose cult had been a serious rival to Christianity in the second century. Heading back for Les Eyzies, I came to the sign again and swung off on a dirt lane that ran between the fields. But when I got to the little park within which the *pigeonnier* presumably was, I found it closed for the season. The signs advertising it, though, would have made the creators of Alley-Oop and the Flintstones blush.

But I found the adjacent village of St.-Leon-sur-Vézère beautifully tranquil, and on the far end of its bridge over the river there sat an inviting café whose terrace looked down on the Vézère and its bordering banks of poplars. Yellow leaves floated languidly downstream on the darkening waters, and in the near distance the village's Romanesque church stood out sharply against a sky that was whitening towards evening.

I shared the terrace with an old man and a girl I took to be his granddaughter, and there was another table of brightly clad hikers, their faces and bare arms tanned and ruddy with good health. On the *cart du vin* there was, among other choices, a 2000 Beaujolais by the glass, and I ordered one, a departure from my custom of sticking to the local products wherever possible. "I do not mind even a bad glass of wine," Alain Querre had told me long ago, "as long as it is an authentic portrait of the people and the place." The Beaujolais wasn't, of course, a portrait of this place, but it wasn't a bad glass, either, and its round, up-front fruit whirled me instantly back to my first visit to France.

That had been in the summer of '65 when I'd come to Paris with my first wife and stayed for a few weeks at a cheap hotel on Boulevard Montparnasse. Beaujolais was all I knew then of French wine, all I bought, until one afternoon the gruff proprietor of the corner *épicerie* (grocery) took pity on my ignorance as I reached for yet another bottle of Beaujolais from his shelves. *"Un moment, mon jeune homme,"* he said, shaking his head at the bottle I had my hand on. Then he said something like, *"Il y a plus de Beaujolais vendu dans ce pays qu'il en est cultivé."* ("There is more Beaujolais sold in this country than there is grown.") Then he led me a few steps to the Bordeaux range where he made a selection for me. I don't recall now if it was more expensive.

I don't drink much Beaujolais these days, quite possibly because of the callow overdoses of those days of almost forty years ago. Whenever I do, however, I'm taken back to Paris, and so it was now. And what I saw in what was both a flashback and a flash-forward, too, was the Café de la Mairie on Place St.-Sulpice, where so often in the past I'd had good luck with my writing. I saw the café's wine-red awning, the terrace with its tiny tables and wicker chairs under the plane trees, the spray of the *place's* fountain over the stone lions crouched about its broad basin, and the great church catching the late afternoon sun on its façade. And seeing all this, I thought of something I heard years ago from the Native American writer Leslie Marmon Silko, when we were talking about places where writing seemed to go best. It was about distance.

"I was never able to write the way I really wanted to about the reservation until I got completely away from it," she told me. "Then, when I was living in Alaska, I found I could see everything. I needed that distance and didn't know it until I had it."

Now I realized that in my own way I was in need of some distance, too. I needed to draw back from the intensity of my encounter with this country, a place of strategic retreat. The Ice Age artists and their audiences hadn't lived in the temple caves but instead at some significant remove from them, and I thought now that I knew at least one of the reasons why. Alaska wouldn't do for me, but Paris always had.

BALZAC VERSUS HITLER

⊱─┼─◆─┼─○─┼─◆─┼─⊰

🐏 Months later when I was back in Santa Fe and told a writer friend that I'd found it necessary to make a strategic retreat to Paris in order to write about my experiences down in Aquitaine, she put her hands to her face in mock horror and sympathy. "How terrible for you!" she exclaimed. In the event, that decision proved a good deal more complicated than it appeared in anecdote, though it had been easy enough to change my plans: to call my son and ask him to meet me in Paris; to get rooms for us at my usual hotel; to drop the Mercedes at the Libourne station and catch the TGV to Gare Montparnasse. All this I could accomplish in an hour on Jean Querre's phone in St.-Crépin. What wasn't so simple was entering Paris after the intensity of Aquitaine, the modern city after the landscape of the deep past.

Even under the best of circumstances the worst way to enter Paris was through the Gare Montparnasse. The station was disorienting, soulless, the second worst idea the municipality ever had, after the destruction of Les Halles. On my rapid way up from Libourne I hadn't had nearly enough time to make the necessary mental transition, and so at the station it felt to me as if I'd gotten off the train while it was still rolling. The city roared and whizzed, its pace as frantic-looking as a disturbed anthill. I couldn't find my balance in it, even after checking into my room at the familiar Hotel de Suede. Notebook in hand, I stumbled the few blocks from the hotel to the Café de la Mairie, the image of which had come so invitingly to mind on the café terrace at St.-Leon-sur-Vézère. But one look at the café and I knew better than to go in there in such a mood. I passed it like the stranger I was, set-tling for a seat on a bench across the *place* where I turned my notebook about in my hands and wondered what the hell I was doing up here. This had been a bad mistake in judgment, a fail-ure of resolve, I felt. I ought to have stayed down there. I should have gone to Régourdou to investigate what evidence was there of a bear cult more than 30,000 years old. I ought to have gone with my son, Charley, down to Niaux to see the Black Salon, which Jean Clottes had recommended to me as a high, consolatory prize for my failure to get into Chauvet Cave. That had been a bogus insight on the café terrace above the river. I'd mistaken normal end-of-day fatigue for cumula-tive psychic overload. Etc.

In such circumstances it's best to try to put some sort of familiar footing under yourself, if you can figure out how to do that. For me in Paris that was simple enough: I'd go over to see Balzac.

On a July afternoon in that summer of '65 when I'd first seen Paris I'd been riding with friends down Boulevard Montparnasse, four of us stuffed into an MG meant for two, and at the intersection of Montparnasse and Boulevard Raspail a white-gloved traffic cop waved us over for just that reason. While that difficulty was being negotiated, I happened to glance up, and there in the leafy shadow of some plane trees was Balzac—Rodin's statute of him—enveloped in a flowing dressing gown turned green and black by time and traffic and all those chimney pots he'd known so well. Behind the statue a tricolor hung limp in the windless day. Nobody else appeared to be taking any note of this phenomenon—just part of the neighborhood—but its effect on me was like a bolt of lightning down through my center; I felt completely lit up from within.

I had already seen some of the city's many marvels but none that hit me like this statue, for here in the heart of the splendid city was a monument to an artist. I knew of nothing like it in my own country where the statues I remembered were of Phil Sheridan, William Tecumseh Sherman, the grave Lincoln, Washington in Roman toga, the heroic heads on Mount Rushmore. Not an artist in the bunch. Here, plainly, was a different cast of culture. Here Art must be held in some special, significant regard. Oh, I'd read about the French and their art, of course, knew my Impressionist history, the ferment of this very Montparnasse neighborhood in the Twenties. But as with Cap Blanc and the Przewalski's horses, seeing was believing back then, too, and this was evidence of a current, continuing reverence for Art, both in the historical figure, Balzac, and the great sculptor who had hammered the image into being and whose work stood in a prominent, public place, reminding passersby to remember. While my friends haggled with the white-gloved cop about the propriety of carrying four in the little car I simply stared at the statue as if my life depended on fixing the image of it in my mind forever. And there, in fact, it has remained, year after year. Whenever I think of Paris, the very essence of its spirit, I don't think of the Eiffel Tower, any of the other monuments, or of the river. I think of Balzac in his robes, staring out of the black caverns of his eyes at the city he so loved.

I couldn't remember, though, ever having come to Balzac needing quite so much. That surely was why I strode to it with such urgency, why I reached up to place my hand on the statue's foot without a trace of self-consciousness, why I stood poised there with the afternoon traffic whizzing past me. What I needed now was some sort of confirmation that I was still on the track of the Life Force as expressed through Art, that in coming up to Paris the only thing that had changed was the venue. And the longer I stood there, gazing up into the eyes, the better I began to feel. I moved slowly about the base, regarding the heroic figure from different angles, the way it seemed to establish suzerainty over its surroundings, to order them into a *composition* in which the statue was centerpiece and focal point of energy. I remembered with astonishing vividness the electric feeling I got when I first beheld this work decades before, and I felt that same energy humming out of it now. It didn't just come from the figure of Balzac, nor even from the artist who'd made the work. It was ultimately from a source that subsumed them both. The metahistorian William Irwin Thompson said in *The Time Falling Bodies Take to Light* that Art is one of the very few ways we have left ourselves to make contact with the sacred. No truer statement, I think, has been made about our current condition, and it was as valid for the obviously mythological cave art as it was for the fictions of Balzac.

It wasn't customary, I knew, to associate the novelist with the sacred: His works are bursting with sexuality in its many manifestations, with appetites and excesses both fictional and literary. No one knew that better than Rodin, who was himself a sort of Balzac-like figure. Before he draped this figure with the robes that were in part a reference to the nightshirt in which the writer always worked, Rodin did several nude studies in which Balzac appears as a rude, untamed natural force with protuberant belly and snout-like penis. I thought of that as I circled the statue, of the fact that Rodin had clearly wanted to have the corporeal lineaments of Balzac there somewhere under the robes of his art and had taken the trouble to hunt up the man who had been Balzac's tailor so that he might have a true sense of the artist's measurements. There had been something even more essential than scrupulosity in this matter, I thought. Rodin might have wanted to make his own, private sort of reference to the fact that whatever the subject matter of the writer's works, Art is *always* related to the sacred, as the corporeal body here was robed with the high calling of literature, which ennobled both the writer and his audience.

Balzac himself appears to have believed this as well: even in his most Rabelaisian mode he felt the presence of the Life Force, in daily life and in his art. Perhaps, now that so much of that world he described in loving detail has vanished, this is the source of his enduring power. With the existential smoke, so to say, of the caves still clinging to my own robes, it was suddenly obvious that I should have made the connection here between Balzac's vanished Paris and the vanished world of the Ice Age, for just as Balzac's novels remain charged in a changed landscape, so and to an even greater degree did those artifacts of the Ice Age. They would remain so, even while we moved steadily away from that time and the phenomena of it.

The roots here are very deep. The human impulse to decorate, to embellish, to create something that hadn't existed before reach back to our very origins and reach outward to what we obscurely know is all about us, the spirit world, which yet defies our clumsy efforts to define it. This was so for the Ice Age artists and no less so for their successors: for Balzac and for Rodin with their earthy appetites; for Bach, for the brilliant, lost Charlie Parker; and for the superficially sacrilegious Henry Miller, who here in this city created a powerful hymn to the human spirit out of the most desperate of materials.

These roots may have put forth their first feelers in the earliest hominids' observations of the rhythms and recurrences of the natural world and the rituals based on these performed by other animals and even insects: the intricate, tail-wagging dance of honey bees, for instance, indicating the direction and distance of a food source from the hive; or the way baboons have been observed patting their hands around the water holes elephants have made with their trunks, as if saying a ritual "Thank you. This is good." Watching such behavior, our ancestors must have concluded that such ritual behavior was the way to best get along. After all, by the time we had finally arrived on earth, the other animals were already here, fully formed and waiting for us. The other animals, then, must have been our first mentors and guides, an enduring truth preserved in folklore from Siberia to the South Pacific, from the caves to the jungle tales of Kipling.

The animals may not have been in themselves guides for Balzac, but when artists of any time or medium create, they are trying to *go back*. They are trying to get in touch with beginnings, with the animals and what lay behind the animals, with what in French is *la source* (the spring, origin, source). The American novelist William Kennedy once spoke about this oblique but essential effort to reach back, to go deep, when he said somewhere that when he went up to his writing room each day, he went there to turn on the tap from which the sacred water might flow. It didn't always happen, he said, and even when it did, you might only get a drop or two from the source. But that was what you worked for and lived for, too—that only occasional, precious contact. The poet and novelist Robert Penn Warren used a different metaphor for the same effort when he remarked that what the writer was always searching for was that "peephole" that would allow him a glimpse of that reality that lay beyond the quotidian plane. In a notebook entry Matisse avoided metaphor altogether and spoke as directly as possible of the effort and its potential reward. Do I believe in God? the artist asked himself, and answered, "Yes, when I work." "When I am submissive and modest," he went on, "I sense myself helped immensely by someone who makes me do things that surpass myself."

The interesting thing in all these instances is the impression conveyed that the artist himself doesn't own or possess the force he wishes to make contact with. It works through him, but it is not his. It is the aspiration to reach back, to go deep, that counts, not ego, not ownership. It is what we feel, however faintly, whenever we are in the presence of genuine Art, whether that of the caves or Corot or John Coltrane. The art needn't be unassailably great, just genuine. At some level then, when we see it or hear it, we, too, believe it because of what it obscurely reminds us. Then, once again, we remember to remember. To remember what is best and truest and most ancient about ourselves.

I didn't know whether my loitering behavior at the statue had been observed by others, and I didn't care, either. I'd gotten what I had come for and turned away from the statue, making my way back to Place St.-Sulpice with a surer step. I crossed Notre-Dame des Champs, where Hemingway had lived while writing his first book of stories. I crossed rue de Fleurus where Gertrude Stein had held her salons with Alice. I cut through the Jardin du Luxembourg with its monuments to Delacroix, its busts of Chopin and Verlaine, and the time-stained statues of the French queens which Faulkner had written so beautifully of in the last lines of *Sanctuary*. Now, suddenly, again, Paris was giving me everything she always had, and, coming to the Place St.-Sulpice, I spotted an empty table at Café de la Mairie, grabbed it, and opened my notebook to write.

What I ended up writing about, however, was not the country of the caves but my experience with Balzac. At that moment, I found nothing wrong with that. Tomorrow I'd return to the matter of the caves and begin filling in the spaces between the cryptic words I'd dashed off down there before I forgot what I had meant and the spaces became silent chasms. What I had yet to understand was that this "strategic retreat" to Paris was not going to be that at all. It was instead to prove a mysteriously-granted new chapter of the same quest that had brought me to Aquitaine, an extension of it into a different place and metaphysical plane, that place and plane of the present we must live in.

The next morning, awaiting Charley, I walked along an edge of the Champ de Mars, bound for the Musée de l'Homme and its exhibits of humanity's imperfectly understood march through time, the weather crisp but with the promise of a later warmth. Past the Ecole Militaire I came to the small glass-and-stone pavilion dedicated to what we have had so little of, in our time or any other—peace. Just then there wasn't much peace even here: a child in a pram was fighting against his mother who, by the look on her face, fully shared his unhappiness. On the pavilion's other side a small group of Japanese men took snapshots of each other posed in front of the glass panels with the prayers inscribed thereon in many languages. They, of course, were representatives from the country that had suffered the ultimate form of war, and their presence was, I felt, testimony to our common hope.

The Musée de l'Homme was housed in one of the two curving wings of the Palais de Chaillot, built for the Paris Exhibition of 1937. I had never cared for its appearance, nor the adjacent Palais de Tokyo: there was a blank facelessness to them quite out of character with so much else about the city. This morning I had to confess that maybe my dislike had at bottom the impression (drawn from a photo) that Hitler had stood on Chaillot's broad terrace with his architect Albert Speer and the sculptor Arno Breker in the dawn hours of June 28, 1940, when he visited Paris as its new ruler. I climbed the steps to the terrace and looked out across the monumental expanse: the Eiffel Tower, the broad green roll of the Champ de Mars, the Ecole Militaire, and to the left of it, the gilded dome of Les Invalides. I tried to avoid looking at the brutal, penile thrust of the Gare Montparnasse, but there it was, right in my sightline. Hitler would have loved it.

Paris was to have been the crown jewel of his empire, and he'd brought Speer with him on that quick tour of inspection so that the architect could see the city's splendors and outdo them in the monolithic monuments he was going create to the Fuhrer in Germany. Hitler himself had something of the artist in him, as he never tired of reminding his flunkies. He was interested in the theater, though chiefly in stagecraft and lighting. He loved Wagner for his use of Nordic mythology. He liked ballet but was uncomfortable with the form-fitting costumes of the dancers. Despite the grandiose architectural schemes he had in mind for Speer to create, however, the highest reach of his imagination was the idea of a stadium that would seat 350,000. In his final two years, he forsook all such decorative projects and their pomp to devote himself exclusively to the work of killing. In the spring of 1944, when it became clear his forces wouldn't be able to hold Paris against the Allied advances, he ordered his general, Dietrich von Choltitz, to blow it all up. Not very long after that, foreseeing the fall of Berlin, he issued similar orders for that city.

Standing where he might once have stood and surrounded by itinerant African street merchants selling bags and other leather goods, it seemed to me that I had a suddenly disclosed view all the way back to the ruins of Oradour-sur-Glane and to that smoking crater in lower Manhattan. Destruction, as has so rightly been said, is always the final despair, the bleak admission that since we cannot have our way, whatever way that is, we shall have Nothing. In the Vietnam War an American officer infamously declared that it had been necessary to destroy a village in order to save it. At the time, some of us found this laughable, but the idea clearly had occurred to desperate others years before. I had to wonder suddenly whether our current war on terror was not almost unconsciously pursuing the same Pyrrhic goal.

Over the summer Alain Querre and I had pondered the meaning of Hitler in an exchange of letters, and I had said that Hitler's ultimate meaning was to remind us of the Destructive Force that lives within the human heart. He was, I thought, unique in history in that he was *wholly* destructive and so in that way darkly illustrative. He too was a part of what had to be remembered as we remembered everything of the human story. Maybe, I said to Querre, the truest thing ever said about Hitler had been said by Albert Speer, who survived both the war and a long imprisonment at Spandau. In the diary he secretly kept during those Spandau years Speer one day wrote that he'd been thinking of how greatly Hitler had lusted to be regarded as a patron of the arts. He was in fact, Speer wrote, just the opposite: He was a grotesque version of the mythic King Midas, "who transformed things not into gold but into corpses."

DEGENERATE ART

⊱⊰

Charley was disappointed to miss the caves but cheerful nonetheless. "Look," I consoled him, "we have ten days together in Paris. Let's do the museums in the mornings, and then I'll work in the afternoons. Worse things have happened." He was a resourceful guy, as he had had to be from an early age, and when I left the hotel in the afternoons for the Café de la Mairie I often heard his guitar chording softly as I passed his room.

That's how we spent those splendid days in Paris, the weather holding beautifully and the city filled, so it seemed, with both sights and events that were so much to my purpose it was as though I was captive to my quest, wherever I might go. In the woods above La Ferrassie I'd had the sudden feeling that I'd been sent to that particular spot, that I could have done no other than what I was doing. Now in Paris I was visited with that same sense, so that instead of feeling that this had been a great mistake, that I ought to have stayed down in

Aquitaine, I now felt that I'd been meant to come up here, that there were things I needed to experience here that would deepen and extend the experiences I'd had.

This began on our first day together when we went to the giant Max Beckmann retrospective at the Pompidou Center. For the western world, forced to face the fact that the mailman might unwittingly deliver powdered poison to your door and that roving the earth were uncountable numbers of those willing to turn their bodies into bombs, this was a grimly appropriate exhibit.

It was brilliantly conceived. Nowhere among the many large rooms filled with the artist's astonishing output was it possible to escape the sounds of warfare emanating from two small theaters that continuously showed grainy footage of the world wars. In the World War I theater, black, sticklike figures ran through a blasted landscape, ducking under barbed wire, tumbling into shell craters, holding onto their rifles for dear life. In the World War II theater, the view was the bombardier's: the ordered flow of the payload earthward where its metallic seed bore the instant blossoms of destruction. The invasion of the soundtracks into the salons was a master stroke, forcing viewers to an understanding of how profoundly war had shaped Beckmann's life and vision.

Gradually, though, you became aware that this condition wasn't just Beckmann's burden; it was in a larger and truer sense the condition of all artists in the modern world—forced over and over again to try to formulate some creative response to warfare that becomes more and more horrific as its technology becomes more ingenious. So, the show wasn't only a Beckmann retrospective. It was a unique retrospective of the world we have made, in which two orders of the imagination compete for the allegiance of the human soul. If, as Daniel Monnier had suggested to me on the banks of the Lot, the artist's work supplies a vital balance against the forces of destruction, that task becomes ever more difficult as technicians and technocrats devise and deploy weapons like dynamite, poison gas, the howitzer, aerial bombs, atomic bombs, hydrogen bombs, smart bombs, and an increasingly vast array of biological weapons. No wonder that in the immediate aftermath of 9/11, the German avant garde composer Karlheinz Stockhausen lamented the composer's inability to compete with the monstrous destructiveness of the 9/11 hijackers. No wonder either that Beckmann portrayed himself in a wild variety of guises—the artist as king, café aristocrat, carnival hand, clown, acrobat, sacrificial victim. Viewed in these rooms with the sounds of war echoing through them, you saw there was a brilliant desperation to his efforts, and as this became increasingly evident you felt that you too shared the artist's travail. This was, of course, the point.

Beckmann had volunteered for service in the medical corps in 1914 with what seems an almost thoughtless glee, writing his wife from the front that the war was a grand opportunity for his art to "gorge" itself on spectacular scenes of destruction. In fairness to him, though, you had to remember that in the beginning many went to that war as to a grand adventure, and the unparalleled realities of the phenomenon were not evident for some months. By 1915 in Belgium, however, Beckmann had come to understand that here was slaughter on a scale the flesh shrank from, that the mind couldn't comprehend. A self-portrait from this time shows a young corpsman at his easel, his face a distorted mask of fear. Soon he suffered a nervous breakdown and was medically discharged.

It might be said he never recovered. He did, though, slowly learn to paint again, beginning at first with scenes of bucolic retreat but gradually assuming a greater, more direct responsibility to depict the world of his time in all its deranged imbalance. If the artist couldn't directly change world affairs, he could at least hold up to "poor deceived humanity" (as Beckmann put it) images of the world's true condition, even as myths had functioned for peoples of the past. By 1933 he had acquired an international reputation, and his work was prominently shown in the art centers of Paris and New York.

But 1933 was also the year the Nazis came to power, and shortly thereafter Beckmann was fired from his teaching sinecure in Frankfort and became one of the targets of the Nazi propaganda machine. Prophetically, that year he completed the triptych *Departure*, perhaps his best-known work, in which he depicts himself as a king being sent into exile, his back turned on home.

Hitler's hatred of Beckmann's work was hardly surprising, because as a failed artist the Fuhrer knew the chthonic power of Art, how deep its roots went. He knew genuine artists could never reliably be conscripted for state purposes—especially for such a state as he had in mind—because their ultimate allegiance was to Art and hence to what lies beneath and beyond Art. Thus their undying threat to the tyrant. It has always been thus, and in our time the persecution of artists by terroristic regimes has been a tellingly conspicuous phenomenon, whether in Nazi Germany, the U.S.S.R., in Falangist Spain, Greece under the colonels, Chile under Pinochet, Afghanistan under the Taliban.

During the Stalinist purges of the 1930s a group of mothers and wives was huddled outside the walls of a prison, awaiting some word of their men being held within. Breaking the numbed silence, a woman asked whether anyone there could describe the situation, and the poet Anna Akhmatova replied, simply, "I can." That seemingly small, singular power is always the threat to massive state terror. Similarly in Falangist Spain, the great writer Miguel de Unamuno dared to publicly answer the speech of a general who predicted his party would soon exterminate their enemies to save the nation. *"Viva la muerte!"* the general cried. "Long live death!" Then Unamuno arose in the hushed university hall. It must be understood, he told his listeners, that such a man as the general was a moral cripple. Cervantes, he said, had been a cripple, too, but not a moral one, whereas this general lacked the "spiritual greatness of a Cervantes" and so was wont to seek "ominous relief in causing mutilation around him." When he left the platform, Unamuno did so as an official enemy of the state, and his last days were spent in that peculiar and special disgrace that is the glory of the genuine artist who has stood up.

In 1937 the Nazis put together a traveling exhibit that drew millions in Munich, Berlin, Vienna, and other captive cities. It was called "Degenerate Art" and featured Beckmann along with Kandinsky, Klee, Oskar Kokoschka, and Ernst Barlach. In the catalogue and in text accompanying their works the artists were savagely ridiculed, but even this was not enough, some thought. They ought, one critic wrote, to be manacled to the museum walls so that good citizens could spit in their faces. The violence of the critical attacks was given more ominous authority by Hitler's threats to sterilize degenerate artists and subject them to criminal prosecution. The artists he wanted about him were men of easy conscience and outsized personal ambition like Speer and Arno Breker. The day the exhibit opened in Munich Beckmann left Germany forever, eventually finding a home in America, where he died in 1950.

The effect of the Beckmann retrospective was so overwhelming in its magnitude, its tragic vision, and its large implications that when Charley and I had gone through its last salon we practically wobbled out into the courtyard of the Pompidou. "That was like looking at a car wreck," he said as we walked across a space that in high summer is an improvised daily exhibition of fire-eaters, fakirs, mimes, acrobats, and wandering scholars. It was quiet now, though, as if in tribute to the exhibition within, only a few students lounging in the hazy sun and a small African drum troupe playing rather softly in one corner. On its other side Charley took another stab at the exhibit's effect on him. "The pictures," he said quietly, "aren't really like nightmares. That's too easy. They're more like fever dreams where everything is turned upside down from normality. When you think about it, that's appropriate because that's how Hitler turned them."

After our immersion in the sounds of war and Beckmann's images of humanity scourged, flayed, fettered, blindfolded, disemboweled, and exiled, I thought we were in need of some re-balancing ourselves, and so I suggested we go right next door to the Fontaine de Stravinsky to look at the sculptures there by Niki de Sainte-Phalle and Jean Tinguely—marvelous, multi-colored, playful things, spouting water jets and mirth in equal measure. "This is part of the story, too," I said at the fountain's edge and talking as much to myself as to Charley. "We need this. Maybe we don't need it any more than that"—jerking my head in the direction of the Pompidou—"but we need it just as much."

Maybe even the war-haunted Beckmann had come to think so. In his final years, when he was awarded an honorary degree from Washington University in St. Louis, he told the students there that they ought to indulge themselves in wine, in explorations of the subconscious, in dancing, joy, melancholy, in all that life had to offer them. But above all, he said, "you should love, love, love!" Surely this was the message also of Niki de Sainte-Phalle's joyous creations, her big-breasted comic mermaid whose nipples were fountains and who appeared to me just then as the esthetic and spiritual descendant of the Venus figurines of the Paleolithic past. And surely, too, this spirit of play and joy had gone into the making of the art of the caves. And love as well, love of the animals and of the earth and of all that life has to offer. These are deep sources, forever beyond the grasp of the destroyers, of whatever stripe.

READING A FORGOTTEN LANGUAGE

At the end of the afternoon the old beauty with her carefully combed white hair and black coat sat on the terrace of the Café de la Mairie. The sun still struck the upper reaches of l'Église Saint-Sulpice and its mismatched towers, but the rest of the *place* was now robed in chilly shadow, and she needed that heavy coat, just as I was glad of the heater in the semi-enclosed portion of the terrace where I sat with my notebook and glass of wine. She had a glass before her as well; I thought it might be Tavel. Whatever it was, she wasn't paying any attention to it, and it might have been ordered only so that she could occupy a table and watch the passing show: the play of light on the waters of the Fontaine des Quatre-Évêques; the big buses belching up and disgorging passengers; pedestrians hurrying home, some with dinner baguettes tucked under arms; neighborhood residents giving dogs their evening airings; couples meeting at the café and quickly sliding into the chairs of newly emptied tables.

From my spot over her shoulder I tried to read the lines of her face, whether they told a tale of slow attrition, of hard-won serenity, of what Melville once called the "pondering repose of if." But I couldn't. There was too much there and I had too little to go on. So I had to be content with her beauty which, though faded, was still substantial. And so, once again, as so often on this journey, Keats's *Ode on a Grecian Urn* forced its way into my consciousness. Before leaving home I'd stapled a copy of it to the back of a notebook where it still hung on, considerably dog-eared and travel-stained. The poem's lines work back and forth between an artful beauty impervious to Time and mortal beauty where Time's ravages come all too swiftly; between maidens painted on an Attic urn and those mortal ones fated to become in time like the old beauty on whom I now gazed. It is one of the great poems in any language on the subject of Art, which was why I'd packed it along, feeling that it would hearten and instruct me at odd moments.

One of those moments had come when I'd said goodbye to Guy de la Valdene outside Bordeaux and driven back toward La Ferrassie. More to break the trip than out of any real hunger I'd stopped at Lalinde, just past Bergerac on the Dordogne, and bought a bottle of mineral water and a baguette and took them to a bench in the town square. There I opened my notebook to the *Ode* and read again the lines about the urn whose beauty is immortal and therefore necessarily mysterious to us. Broad brown leaves, ubiquitous reminders of Time and its seasons, skittered past my feet in a mild breeze, and in this post-lunch lull I had the place almost to myself, except for two teenagers who eyed me skeptically from the shade of the market shed.

The young men seemed to be trying to assess me: Who was this foreign old fart reading something in a notebook and tearing off chunks of a baguette to feed the sparrows with an absent-minded generosity? They could hardly have guessed of course that what had just occurred to me was an analogy between Keats's painted urn and the art of the caves: both were picture languages, but the languages themselves had been lost to Time's slow drift, and thus their meanings were tantalizingly obscure. We knew only, it seemed, that there was meaning in them, and great meaning too, meaning that held some vitally necessary significance for us as members of the human race. It was more than a riddle, which always involves a kind of trick, it seems to me. And it was more than a matter of cracking a code as the brilliant Champollion had done with Egyptian hieroglyphics. Rather, it was as if in both the painted procession of the figures on the urn and those etched or painted on the cave walls we sensed the nearness of the DNA of the universe—what it all meant. But there was too much blackness surrounding the figures—context, maybe—and so the story the figures told was tantalizing fragmentary. In that placid moment in Lalinde it seemed to me that I sat within the narrowest needle of light, surrounded by the darkness of the long, unknowable past, like those carefully positioned lights in the caves that illuminated only fragments of the vast whole. Where else on earth, I wondered, glancing up from Keats's lines, could you be so intimately aware of this existential condition as here in this country with its multiple sites (Lalinde was one of them) at which humankind had marked its earliest understanding of how things were on earth? This sunny square ringed by shops, autos, the clock tower, all seemed suddenly chimerical and evanescent in comparison with the dark yet luminous past.

Once, Egypt and Greece and Rome had been Western civilization's official metaphors for the past. But all these civilizations were comparative latecomers, moderns that stood on the shaggy shoulders of the Paleolithic peoples. And when the existence of the earlier peoples was discovered in the mid-nineteenth century and their artistic achievements publicized, it was revolutionary. Our notions of antiquity were rudely overturned, and quite suddenly vast chasms of chronological blackness yawned. The world was far older than had been imagined and humankind's story far different from when Napoleon drove into Egypt and sought to awe his troops by telling them that forty centuries looked down on their deeds. Here in Lalinde forty centuries were nothing, and even the antiquity of Keats's urn in this moment looked a trifle out of order.

But that view of the *Ode* had been but momentary, and in Paris Keats had been very much with me. This morning, when Charley and I had gone to the Louvre to look at the Greek amphorae, the poet was there once again as we looked at the ochre-colored figures of helmeted hoplites, close-cropped maidens, and sacrificial animals. "What men or gods are these?" the poet had asked.

What maidens loth?
What mad pursuit? What struggle to escape?
What pipes and timbrels? What wild ecstasy?

What indeed? "A lot of what's going on here we really don't know that much about," I said to Charley as we moved slowly around the amphorae in their glass cases. "These are pictures of stories—or they're references to stories. Kind of like a shorthand the Greeks of that time would've been able to read, because they already knew the stories. Keats says we have to simply surrender to them. We have to surrender to them as objects of beauty and forget about our ignorance: 'Beauty is truth, truth beauty—that is all / Ye know on earth, and all ye need to know.'" Sons inevitably find different heroes than their fathers, and since he only nodded politely I couldn't tell whether or not he had surrendered to Keats's lines.

Of course, the lines had become a cliché, the ultimate left-handed tribute Time pays to something perfectly put. But such a development doesn't make the expression any less true, unless time and usage have worn away its patina of felicity and revealed something rather ordinary and drab beneath. That hadn't happened with Keats's lines, not for me, anyway, though now in college English classes they may be granted their enduring status less as truth than as a license almost archaic.

But truth is what they are. The beauty of the images of myth, whether on Attic urns or the limestone walls of caves, is inetricable from their truth. In making them, the now-anonymous artists had been working as closely as possible to the sacred sources, to those things that may only be expressed by symbolic indirection. They had known the grammar and vocabulary of the now-forgotten language of myth, and as they articulated it in images the Life Force worked through their fingers as unmistakably as a willow's buds breaking their dark scales in spring.

The ancient audiences would have implicitly assented to the simultaneously expressed truth and beauty of the graven images without feeling the need to know more about them than what was so perfectly manifest there. As Charley and I moved around the display cases, scrutinizing the urns from this angle and that, I was unpleasantly reminded of the de-mythicizing habit of the human mind and wondered where it ultimately came from. In the Old Testament Yahweh thunder-ously refuses to give in to it, answering man's question about His identity, "I am that I am." That later readers could find these words cryptic traces the path that leads from mytholog-ical belief to rationalized religion. More than half of any god, it has rightly been said, must remain a mystery. Put another way, a god who is fully known is no longer a god, and we our-selves know that when the Greeks and Romans had fully expli-cated and rationalized their gods, the gods died, and their graves were pointed out to the idle and curious.

The process of de-mythicizing gods and heroes can be said, of course, to have the same origins as the ability to sym-bolize and depict them in the first place: the human brain with its almost fabulous combination of archaic brain stem and bulging frontal lobes. In our time the very term "myth," which once meant Beautiful Truth, now signifies that which has been exposed as a falsehood. We insist on knowing *everything* about our gods and heroes and on prying beneath the images of divinity to get at what we foolishly imagine is the "truth." In l'Eglise Saint-Sulpice, just across the *place* from the café where I now sat, there was a large photograph of the dead Christ as revealed by the modern magic of x-rays of the Shroud of Turin. This must be an appeal to modern Christian sensibility that wants confirmation of Christ's historicity. To less-evolved worshippers, those attuned to Christ's mythological significance, it must appear as nothing less than an appalling blasphemy. Surely, this is the *reductio ad absurdum* of that prying, rationalizing impulse that killed off belief in the older figures of divinity. It is only slightly more awful than the recent Protestant reinvention of Jesus as Everybody's Pal.

When at last I left the café the stream of the homeward bound had dwindled. There were more empty tables on the terrace and more of those like myself who had sought the comfort of the heaters of the semi-enclosed section. The shadows had completely enveloped the church, and the jets of the fountain had become the color of pewter in the dying light. Still, the old beauty sat on before her glass of wine, nursing it as she may have been nursing her memories. She was old enough, I judged, to have seen it all, as we say: the Great Depression when ordinary Parisians slept out on the portico of the Bourse; the fall of France and the Occupation; Algeria and de Gaulle's triumphant return to power; the vandalizing of the city by Pompidou; the new age of the terrorist. . . . She didn't seem to be at all captive to some senescent trance but instead attuned to something not evident, listening maybe like the Venus figure of Laussel. "Heard melodies are sweet," Keats wrote, "but those unheard / Are sweeter. . . ."

IN THE HALL OF THE PAST

For me there has always been something slightly shabby about the Jardin des Plantes complex. The gardens themselves are lovely in all seasons, a great spot for a leisurely stroll or a picnic. And over the years I have seen some wonderful exhibitions in its Galerie de Mineralogie; I remember in particular one celebrating the life of that searcher after the wild spirit of divinity, Théodore Monod, who is too little known in America. But the zoo is a disgrace, and many of the other galleries seem to remain shuttered for years at a stretch. Even when it reopened after a long *fermeture* the Galerie de Paléontologie et Anatomie Comparée had a down-at-heels dustiness to it, the ancient bones of the specimen creatures looking not only all of their years but neglected as well, and the bodies of long-dead things floating in ghastly suspension in bottles of formalin.

Yet on one of our last days in Paris I'd wanted Charley to see a few of the exhibits in there and to be reminded of them myself. So, as if we were indeed the lords of creation instead of merely two of its creatures, we strolled through the high hall as through eons: past the articulated skeletons of giant saurians that had lumbered over the planet when ferns were giants, too; past whales, giants of the deep that long preceded humankind and now were threatened by it; past the great apes; past the stuffed foot of a mammoth, discovered in Siberia in 1901 and still retaining some wisps of reddish hair. And then mammoth skeletons with their huge, sinuous tusks, and one of a cave bear standing erect, the *Ursus spelaeus* the Ice Age peoples knew and feared and doubtless worshipped as well.

Some find the evidence of Ice Age bear cults dubious, and it's always dangerous to argue for the antiquity of any cultural practice based on manifestations of it at later dates and different places. Yet the clear evidence of bear cults in so many cultures combines tellingly with symbolic arrangements of bear bones and skulls in the caves that it is hard to imagine that Paleolithic peoples didn't worship these creatures and regard them as tutelary beings who in their peculiarly humanoid carriage stood at the threshold between all the other animals and humankind. The bear's special power and position in the pantheon is strongly suggested by the care various peoples took to avoid naming it directly. To some he was Old Man; to others, Winter Sleeper; and to still others, the Four-Legged Hunter. Then there was the even more removed circumlocution, That's Him. Standing in the shadow of the great being, That's Him reared up on his bent hindquarters, was a moving, oddly unsettling experience for us, as if after all the thousands of years since it had last drawn breath, the bear still wished to tell us something, the whitened, polished bones wired together, the fanged mouth opened to speak, if only we could stop chattering about ourselves long enough to listen.

One of the persistent themes of world folklore is that once, in the morning of the world, humans had understood the languages of the other animals. The loss of this ability is symbolic of the exile from the paradisal state of unindividuated harmony, and in the myths its reacquisition is never general—we can't go back as a species—but only individual and exceptional. But surely if the cave bears could speak to us and we could understand them, they would tell us, "You're making a big mistake. Life is not as you think it is: It is much closer to what your ancient ancestors believed when they drew our outlines in the caves."

Those ancestors had seen divinity shining out of the creatures they knew. Most likely, they had seen it also in other aspects of earthly life—rocks, springs, the stars—though the evidence we have thus far speaks chiefly of the animals. This sense of theirs, that the earth and its creatures were instinct with soul life, eventually came to be regarded as the single most distinguishing characteristic of the savage state. Seeing beyond it, seeing it as a "myth," was what freed us to dominate the planet and to rearrange it to our perceived needs, draining the swamps, straightening rivers, mowing down the groves, casually exterminating animal species.

But the costs of our triumph have been as heavy for us as for the earth, and just as the animals are smaller in size and far fewer in number since the days of the cave bear, so our sense of life has become radically diminished. At the same time and because of this, our fear of death has become so overwhelming that there is virtually nothing humankind will not try in the vain hope of avoiding it. Arranging to be hung upside down in a vat of liquid nitrogen until a cure can be found for what killed us is a stratagem that could only occur to a species that has lost the belief in the necessary interconnectedness of all things, most especially Life and Death—that savage understanding the caveman artists possessed.

High above where Charley and I stood, up there where the light from the dirty windows poured in yellow-brown shafts down over the archaic forms of life, there was a reproduction of a portion of a wall of Lascaux, the running animals, bulls, horses, deer, done with a crudeness not in keeping with the fabulous original. Still, I thought it was a nice touch here. I pointed it out to Charley and said the deer reminded me of the exhibit I'd wanted to save for last: the antlered skull of a megaloceros, the giant deer of the Ice Age. I'd come across it once by accident when prowling about the neglected reaches of the hall late on a weekday afternoon. There it was, bolted to a badly peeling stretch of wall, a forgotten artifact in an upper-story stairwell with only a couple of empty display cases for company.

It deserved far better. From tip to tip its antlers went a good ten feet and at their greatest width must have measured two feet across. When Charley and I climbed up to see it, I was struck again by its majesty, almost its anatomical implausibility, for even so huge a neck and body would have been taxed, I thought, to support such a tree of antler. The eye sockets stared blackly down at us across millennia, and my neck hairs bristled when I thought of how defenseless humans must have

felt in the presence of such a creature–and all the other creatures of that wilderness time and place.

Both Neanderthals and Cro-Magnons would have known
the megaloceros, though it was never found in the profligate
numbers the reindeer once were, and from a strictly economic
point of view it might have been prized mainly for the amount
of horn a single creature could yield to hunters who had
learned how to fashion cunning implements and ornaments
from such material. I wanted suddenly to touch those antlers,
but my arms were too short and the antlers remained out of
reach. The best I could do was move up a couple of steps from
the stairwell and reach out to the bones of the nasal passages.
Once, long ago, my kind and its kind had breathed the common air of earth, and now in this moment we did so again, in
my imagination. I saw the hunters stalking the grand creature
through snowdrifts or across a windy, gray tundra, saw the
shafts strike home, the smoking blood spilled, and the hunters'
prayers and invocations. Here for certain was one of those
powerful images of which Robert Penn Warren had once spoken, an image that allowed you what he thought of as a "peephole" onto Reality and to which you could return again and
again as the need arose. The skull did that for me at that
moment and subsequently, allowing me a vivid glimpse into
that world of ice, antlers, and artists that I had been trying for
many months to enter.

I told Charley about the reindeer I'd seen in Font-de-
Gaume, about how they were for the Cro-Magnons apparently
the economic equivalent of what the buffalo had been for the
Plains tribes of America. Which brought to mind a theory that

the great art of the caves had been dependent on the surplus of these creatures. I didn't buy it, I said, finding it a gross simplification.

Economic factors can never sufficiently account for the activity of the imagination, and in any case the Cro-Magnon hunters who created the art had lived on Saiga antelope, steppe bison, wild oxen, woolly mammoths, horses, and the megaloceros as well as the vast herds of reindeer. There seems no doubt that from ±35,000 years ago to ±10,000 years ago there was sufficient game from all these sources for the small groups of hunters to live well. Reasoning from these facts, some paleontologists theorize that the rise of the high art of the Magdalenian period was built on the solid foundation of this relative prosperity. The evidence of the caves tells us, they say, that these people did not have to spend all of their waking hours chasing game. Some members of the groups, in other words, could be spared from the work of the hunt to create art. Art, so the logic of this argument runs, is built on leisure. No economic surplus, no leisure. No leisure, no art. And the argument seems successfully closed when it's pointed out that with the final retreat of the ice caps the great herds drifted northward and the days of the surplus ended—and so did the period of the high art. Life became harder then. The hunters had to go ever farther afield for game. Permanent encampments became increasingly impractical, and as they did, regular access to the cave sanctuaries was no longer possible. Thus the lines of transmission necessary for the maintenance of the great tradition became increasingly attenuated until finally they snapped, and the art of the Cro-Magnons degenerated into a crude caricature of its ancient magnificence. This ±8,000 years ago.

But what is crucially left out of this argument is what robs it of its validity—the mysterious, ultimately irrepressible workings of the imaginative impulse. These, to be sure, are not nearly as well understood as humankind's economic activities, but they are basic to our nature nevertheless and are in fact coeval with it. Moreover, this argument has the terribly misleading tendency to make Art into a leisure activity dependent on the hard, practical work of non-artists. Nothing could be further from the truth.

In the first place, the origins of Art vastly pre-date the age of game surpluses in northern Europe. Even if we confine ourselves to that region and its theoretical "creative explosion" of artistic activity during the Upper Paleolithic period, it is doubtful that the artists of the caves were spared "real work" so that they could play at decoration. It is much more likely that their work was regarded as *so essential* to the healthy balance of the groups that they were regarded as specialists, technicians of the sacred, for whom strictly economic activity would have been distinctly secondary. The work of the chase was the work of killing: life fed on death. No predominantly hunting culture could ever have avoided that daily realization. So, the work of the artists restored the vital balance by celebrating the numinous lives of the animals necessary for human life. Here was another illustration of what Daniel Monnier had pointed out to me on that sunny day on the Lot when we stood, emotionally speaking, in the long shadow of the story of Pierre Fournié's execution at the hands of the SS. Maybe it was the supreme illustration because it came so early in the modern human story.

And then there is the further fact that Art didn't disappear with the reindeer. It only changed forms, like the fabulous shape-shifters of myth. The imaginative impulse survived the environmental changes of the ending of the Ice Age to re-emerge in the art of the Neolithic Revolution that followed. And it has survived every other crisis, natural or manmade. It survived the savagery and pillaging of the Crusades, the Black Death, the periodic rapine inflicted on Europe by nomadic invaders, the advent of global warfare and weapons of mass destruction.

It survived the best efforts of the Nazis, too, and their failed artist, Hitler, and art thief, Hermann Göring. In this connection, I remember seeing in Paris some years ago an exhibit of art from the death camps, at the Memorial to the Unknown Jewish Martyr. What struck me about it was the tenderness — the exquisite tenderness, really — of some of the watercolors. These were scenes, after all, of the camps with their barracks, their barbed wire and guard towers. Yet the treatment of this ghastly landscape was ultimately loving because the artists knew they had triumphed over the facts of the camps through making images of them. It was not great art, only genuine, which always confers its special sort of greatness, whatever the circumstance, whatever the stony soil.

ST.-SULPICE

A decade ago a couple of journalistic assignments brought me to France and to Paris, where I stayed at a small hotel on the Place St.-Sulpice. I'd always wanted to try the Hotel Recamier, snugged into a quiet corner of the *place* with a fine view of the fountain and the church, and with immediate access to the Café de la Mairie.

Recamier had location—but no air-conditioning worthy of the name. And so on several very hot July nights I found myself sitting out by the fountain and taking a weary pleasure in its cool splashings. The grand front of the church was lighted: its double row of columns, its five flights of steps, and above these its mismatched towers, visual evidence that the church's last architect had run out of funding. It was on one of those nights out there that I realized with something of a jolt that this church, *my* church, was actually rather ugly: asymmetrical, bulbous, imposing, but not really powerful in presence as Notre Dame is or La Madeleine.

Still, it was my church and had been years before I'd first seen it. Back in high school a culturally advanced friend had loaned me an LP recording of E. Power Biggs playing the organ at St.-Sulpice, and the experience was formative. One of the things I made certain to do in that summer when I first saw Paris was to go over to the church, and I have been attending mass there ever since, whenever I'm in the city.

This has mostly been, I must confess, so that I could hear Daniel Roth on the legendary Chalgrin organ, one of the world's larger ones at 6,588 pipes, particularly his improvisations on sacred music at the end of formal services. Gradually, though, through the years my appreciation of the services had widened a bit to include the choral interludes, the expressive, long-armed gestures of the choir director, even the smell of the censer ceremoniously waved over the congregation. You still couldn't class me as a convert, but maybe in the long, patient gaze of Latin Catholicism the Church might think I was coming right along. After all, it has been playing the waiting game with heathens almost since the conversion of Constantine.

Now on the morning of the last day of my quest, here I was once more, sitting well back in the ranks of the narrow, straight-backed chairs that have always struck me as more formal somehow than the joined pews I knew from the casual churchgoing of my childhood. And as the clerics took their turns at the high altar and several young boys read Scripture and the long-armed choir director waved his hands over the choir, marking the cadences of the responses, it came to me that here too was a kind of cave.

The mythographer Joseph Campbell somewhere said that the temple caves were the landscape of the human soul, and on this mellow morning I felt his metaphor ought to be extended to include churches such as this. Not all churches, though, would do. The kind of church I had in mind had to be old and time-stained. No recent, red-brick one would do with marquee out front, panhandling passersby, like one I passed in Florida where the sign read, "Come On In! Beat The Heat!" Nor could the building look as if it might with certain modifications serve as the national headquarters of an insurance company or a college fraternity. No, the kind of church I thought could fit the metaphor must bear the marks of time. It must be high-ceilinged, deep, made of stone, echoing. It must, in other words, resemble a cave. It must feel like one, and smell like one, too. It must strike you on entering as a sacred place, which, as William Irwin Thompson so well put it, is one that connects our creaturely concerns to the whole of creation.

Such a structure is a place to which we can confidently come, bringing to it our full and flawed humanity, knowing that here it will be both comprehended and subsumed in the grand drama that is existence. All this was what so often I'd felt inside St.-Sulpice but never articulated to myself until this morning. It was what the building's ponderous mass encouraged, even as that of the caves once had: this vast, dim, dingy space, lined about with chapels within whose reaches ragged women and men—*clochards* they once were called—slept, surrounded by their precious bundles; where old women knelt in murmuring supplication to the Virgin; where African missionaries made pilgrims' progress around the stations of the cross while bright-shirted tourists snapped photos of them; and where a few pigeons and sparrows roosted in the rearward heights and were startled into flight when Daniel Roth played the organ, shaking everything under heaven.

On the worn, uneven stones of the church's floor there ran a strip of bronze, from north to south along the transept. It ended at an obelisk that was topped with a metallic globe. On the equinoxes they say a ray of sunlight from the high windows is guided along this strip to the globe where its reflection illuminates an adjacent cross. I have never witnessed this miracle but am encouraged to believe it by almost everything in here. And there was also in here the Chapel of the Angels, just to your right as you entered off the *place*, decorated with a now-dim fresco by Delacroix, of Jacob wrestling with the angel. I had long interpreted the fresco as the artist's struggle with his muse. On this day, though, I saw it as a depiction of humankind's beautiful but bruising engagement with the Life Force that blesses us—but always at a cost.

All this and much more was present and available to me now, and to all the others around me, some of whom I exchanged handshakes with at the end of services as the clerics filed past us towards the heavy doors. In this moment, all of us, I felt, stood in a sacred place, one prepared for by the long, luminous existence of the temple caves. It was in the caves that we first understood there were places to which we could come, carrying the burden of our common humanity with all its contradictions, the small, secret wars between the

Life Force and the Destructive Impulse, fought daily across the invisible field of the soul and made manifest in small acts of compassion, small weaknesses of spite.

But above all else, it was the organ, its music, investing the building and its parishioners with the sound of the sacredness of everyday life. The artist, invisible to us in the organ loft, did for all below what the artists of the caves had done for our ancestors, making us aware that we are *always* in the presence of the sacred, every day, and that there is no escape from it. As he rolled the great instrument I felt the old building grate on its axis, its massive masonry moving in answer to the peals and thunder tones. Here was an assault of beauty, endured by the stones, the stained glass windows, the pigeons, and parishioners. So here It was, once again and always, showering down on us through the crepuscular, polluted air trapped within the walls of this special cave: air stained with centuries'-old incense and candle drippings; stale breath and stealthy farts; the profanations of incomplete or wholly fraudulent confessions; whispers of priestly seductions; last night's dried lust and this morning's bitter coffee; the faint scent of the deep ranks of Easter flowers past and the belches of those buses that in 1942 had carried the Jews to the Vélodrome, from which they departed for the camps and the gas chambers; air now completely filled with music, Art, that comprehended all this and gathered it up in the triumph of affirmation.

The notes were the coda, powerful, beautiful, unmistakably assertive, to a process that had begun for me the moment I'd heard the news of the first plane to hit the towers on 9/11;

that had taken on tone and definition in my Santa Fe study when I'd seen the Cro-Magnon skull once again and placed my hand on the pages of the book about Chauvet Cave; that had taken me deep into the earth at Rouffignac and brought me out again to a place I thought I already knew so well. But now I understood it to be the ground of confirmation of what I had thought was true but had never so clearly seen: that we have been placed on this spinning blue ball and meant to love it and to love one another, as best we're able. Meant to laugh and sing and dance; to drink wine; and to glory in acts of the imagination that help us to remember to remember all of this.

We will never fully decipher the silent symphonic dance of the Ice Age art, and that's just as it should be, its mysteries a continuing reproof to our arrogance. Defended by a stout little army of functionaries, ticket-takers, souvenir sellers, guides; bolted behind gates and doors; connected by key-pads to local constabularies; fenced off by dripping railings and rusted mesh screens; being slowly swallowed by earth and the hairy reach of roots, the casual detritus of Time: still the awesome art gestures towards us. The bear hunches and prowls. The horse gallops. The old rhino lowers his bent-horned head. The bison charges: all impervious to Time's incursions—and ours.

ACKNOWLEDGMENTS

I have always found it a special sort of pleasure to acknowledge the help friends have so generously given me in the making of my books. Your friends are your creative context, Gary Snyder once remarked, and certainly my books could never have been written without the intelligent and patient suggestions of so many friends, through so many years. Had I been capable of acting more thoroughly on their advice, I have no doubt the books would be better than they are.

So it is with this latest work. And here I have particularly to thank Alain Querre, who was so tirelessly helpful at every stage of the project: suggesting itineraries, making contacts, sending useful books and pamphlets, reading drafts. More than any of these invaluable services, though, it has been of the greatest importance for me to have had the opportunity to talk with him about everything under the sun—and under the earth as well. I want also to thank Sheila Querre for her special friendship and graceful hospitality. The tranquil haven of her home was crucial to me at various stages of my travels in the land of the temple caves.

Peter Nabokov, David S. Whitley, Gendron Jensen, and Merloyd Lawrence lent important books and even more important advice. My wife, Elise R. Turner, listened to the various drafts by our fireside and thus provided that earliest sense of audience. This is certainly a better book for their help, though they are, of course, in no way responsible for its shortcomings of vision and expression.

I wish it were practical to thank all of the following friends in individual detail, but it is not. My hope is that each will believe me when I say that I remember well the gifts they so freely gave: Raphiel Benjamin, Mélanie Benoit, Barbara Burn, Kay Carlson, Jean Clottes, Jeanie P. Fleming, Mahmoud Hamadani, Peg Johnson, Diane Karp, David Kronen, W.S. Merwin, Karen Milstein, Philip Milstein, Nancy Newhouse, Deanne K. Newman, Eugene Newmann, John Purdie, Danielle Querre, Jean Querre, Nicole Querre, Noel Querre, Bill Sayre, Sam Scott, Ronald Sheffler, Robin Straus, Erik Trinkaus, Aaron B. Turner, Charles F. Turner, Charles H. Turner, Guy de la Valdene.

REFERENCES

Aisenberg, Nadya (ed.). *We Animals: Poems of Our World* (San Francisco: Sierra Club Books, 1989).

Aitken, Robert. "Massacre at Oradour-sur-Glane: 2nd Waffen SS Panzer Das Reich Division's Crime and Punishment." *Litigation* (Fall 1999).

American Museum of Natural History. *The First Europeans: Treasures from the Hills of Atapuerca* (New York: American Museum of Natural History, 2003).

Baruchello, Gianfranco, and Henry Martin. *How to Imagine: A Narrative on Art, Agriculture and Creativity* (Toronto: Bantam Books, 1984, 1985).

Bleibtreu, John N. *The Parable of the Beast* (Toronto: Collier-Macmillan, 1968, 1969).

Campbell, Joseph. *The Masks of God: Primitive Mythology* (New York: Viking Press, 1959, 1970).

————. *The Way of the Animal Powers; Historical Atlas of World Mythology*, Vol. 1 (London: Summerfield Press, 1983).

Ceram, C. W. *Gods, Graves, and Scholars: The Story of Archaeology* (Toronto, New York, London: Bantam Books, 1951, 1972).

Chauvet, Jean-Marie, et al. *Dawn of Art: The Chauvet Cave* (New York: Harry N. Abrams, 1995, 1996).

Cohen, Claudine. *The Fate of the Mammoth: Fossils, Myth, and History*, trans., William Rodarmor (Chicago, London: University of Chicago Press, 2002).

Count, Earl W. "Myth as World View: A Biosocial Synthesis," in Stanley Diamond (ed.), *Culture in History: Essays in Honor of Paul Radin* (New York: Columbia University Press, 1960).

Davenport, Guy. "Prehistoric Eyes," in Davenport, *The Geography of the Imagination* (San Francisco: North Point Press, 1981).

Dubos, René. *The Wooing of Earth: New Perspectives on Man's Use of Nature* (New York: Charles Scribner's Sons, 1980).

Eckstein, Gustav. *The Body Has a Head* (New York, Evanston, and London: Harper & Row, 1969, 1970).

Farmer, Sarah. *Martyred Village: Commemorating the Massacre at Oradour-sur-Glane* (Berkeley, Los Angeles, London: University of California Press, 1999).

Flam, Jack (ed.). *Matisse on Art* (Berkeley, Los Angeles: University of California Press, 1995).

Freud, Sigmund. *Beyond the Pleasure Principle*, trans., James Strachey (New York: Bantam Books, 1928, 1972).

Graves, Robert. *The Greek Myths*, Vol. 1 (Harmondsworth, England, Baltimore: Penguin Books, 1955, 1973).

Herbert, Zbigniew. *Barbarian in the Garden*, trans., Michael March and Jaroslaw Anders (New York, San Diego: Harcourt Brace, 1962, 1985).

Isaacs, Glynn, and Richard E. F. Leakey. *Human Ancestors* (San Francisco: W. H. Freeman, 1960, 1979).

Jung, C. J. *The Spirit in Man, Art, and Literature*, trans., R. F. C. Hull (Princeton: Princeton University Press, 1966, 1972).

Kershaw, Ian. *Hitler: 1936–1945: Nemesis* (New York: W. W. Norton, 2000).

La Barre, Weston. *The Ghost Dance: The Origins of Religion* (New York: A Delta Book, 1970, 1972).

Leroi-Gourhan, André. *Treasures of Prehistoric Art*, trans., Norbert Guterman (New York: Harry N. Abrams, n.d.).

Lewis-Williams, David. *The Mind in the Cave: Consciousness and the Origins of Art* (London: Thames & Hudson, 2002).

Manes, Christoper. *Other Creations: Recovering the Spirituality of Animals* (New York, London, Toronto, Sydney, Auckland: Doubleday, 1977).

Marnham, Patrick. *Resistance and Betrayal: The Death and Life of the Greatest Hero of the French Resistance* (New York: Random House, 2000).

Miller, Henry. *Remember to Remember* (New York: New Directions, 1947).

Nietzsche, Friedrich. *The Birth of Tragedy* in *The Philosophy of Nietzsche*, trans. and ed., Clifton Fadiman (New York: Modern Library, n.d.).

Nora, Pierre. "Between Memory and History," trans., Marc Roudebush. *Representations*, No. 26 (Spring 1989).

Otto, Walter F. *Dionysus, Myth and Cult*, trans., Robert B. Palmer (Bloomington, Indiana, London: Indiana University Press, 1933, 1965).

Ovid. *Metamorphoses*, trans., Mary M. Innes (Harmondsworth, England, Baltimore: Penguin Books, 1955, 1973).

Payne, Katy. *Silent Thunder: In The Presence of Elephants* (New York: Simon & Schuster, 1998).

Price, T. Douglas, and Anne Birgitte Gebauer (eds.). *Last Hunters, First Farmers: New Perspectives on the Prehistoric Transition to Agriculture* (Santa Fe, New Mexico: School of American Research Press, 1995).

Restale, Richard. *The Mind* (Toronto, New York, London, Sydney, Auckland: Bantam Books, 1988).

Rilke, Rainer Maria. *Letters on Cézanne*, trans., Joel Agee (New York: Fromm International Publishing, 1985).

Schnapp, Alain. *The Discovery of the Past*, trans., Ian Kinnes and Gillian Varndell (New York: Harry N. Abrams, 1997).

Schulz-Hoffman, Carla, and Judith C. Weiss. *Max Beckmann: Retrospective* (New York, London: W. W. Norton, 1984).

Shepard, Paul. *The Tender Carnivore & The Sacred Game* (Athens, Georgia: University of Georgia Press, 1973, 1998).

Sobin, Gustaf. *Luminous Debris: Reflecting on Vestige in Provence and Languedoc* (Berkeley, Los Angeles, London: University of California Press, 1999).

Speer, Albert. *Spandau: The Secret Diaries*, trans., Richard and Clara Winston (New York: Macmillan, 1976).

Tattersall, Ian. *The Last Neanderthal: The Rise, Success, and Mysterious Extinction of Our Closest Human Relatives*, revised edition (Boulder: Westview Press, 1999).

Thompson, William Irwin. *The Time Falling Bodies Take to Light: Mythology, Sexuality, & the Origins of Culture* (New York: St. Martin's Press, 1981).

Toms, Michael. "The Ancient Powers of the Soul." *IONS: Noetic Sciences Review* (June-August 2002).

Ucko, Peter J., and Andrée Rosenfeld. *Paleolithic Cave Art* (New York, Toronto: McGraw-Hill, 1967, 1973).

Vialou, Denis. *Prehistoric Art and Civilization*, trans., Paul G. Bahn (New York: Harry N. Abrams, 1998).

Watts, Alan. *Tao: The Watercourse Way* (New York: Pantheon Books, 1975).

Webster, Paul. *Petain's Crime: The Full Story of French Collaboration in the Holocaust* (Chicago: Ivan R. Dee, 1991).

White, Randall. *Prehistoric Art: The Symbolic Journey of Humankind* (New York: Harry N. Abrams, 2003).

Whitley, David S. *The Art of the Shaman: Rock Art of California* (Salt Lake City: University of Utah Press, 2000).

———."Three Days at Chauvet: A Look at the World's Oldest Art" (unpublished paper).